Rufus Phineas Stebbins

A Study of the Pentateuch for Popular Reading

being an inquiry into the age of the so-called books of Moses

Rufus Phineas Stebbins

A Study of the Pentateuch for Popular Reading
being an inquiry into the age of the so-called books of Moses

ISBN/EAN: 9783337169565

Printed in Europe, USA, Canada, Australia, Japan

Cover: Foto ©Lupo / pixelio.de

More available books at **www.hansebooks.com**

A

STUDY OF THE PENTATEUCH.

FOR POPULAR READING.

BEING AN INQUIRY INTO THE AGE OF THE SO-CALLED BOOKS OF MOSES, WITH AN INTRODUCTORY EXAMINATION OF RECENT DUTCH THEORIES, AS REPRESENTED BY DR. KUENEN'S "RELIGION OF ISRAEL."

BY

RUFUS P. STEBBINS, D.D.

Formerly President, Lecturer on Hebrew Literature, and Professor of Theology in the Meadville Theological School.

BOSTON:
GEO. H. ELLIS, 141 FRANKLIN STREET.
1883.

PREFACE.

THIS work is substantially a reprint of articles published in the *Unitarian Review*, 1879 and 1880. I have not found it necessary to essentially modify any of the arguments there presented in the present publication. Several works and many articles, at home and abroad, have since been published; but they do not in the slightest degree affect the force of the argument presented in the following "Study."

It seemed better to give the criticism on the Dutch school as represented by Dr. Kuenen as originally written than to attempt by partial rewriting and voluminous notes to introduce the substance of it into the body of the work. In this manner, the argument of the "Study" is not interrupted by noticing the objections and answering the arguments and criticising the evidence which are offered by many writers as well as by Dr. Kuenen. Professor W. Robertson Smith's lectures on the *Old Testament and the Jewish Church* were not published till this work was more than half through the press. I have examined it with care, and find very little which would have required any notice, had I received it in season. Though he takes substantially the same ground on many points as the Dutch school, he denies that Deuteronomy is a forgery of the priests of the time of Josiah, and that the Books of the Chronicles are historical forgeries to sustain the new claims of the priesthood. The three principal reasons which he gives for the late origin of the Pentateuch, especially the ritual portion of it, are: first, the neglect of observing the law and direct violations of it down to the division of the kingdom or later; second, a distinct priestly family or caste did not exist till the time of Ezra; and, third, the early prophets, Amos, Hosea, Isaiah, and Micah, refer to no written law, and denounce ritual observances. I have examined with care whether the evidence adduced to sustain these reasons is sufficient to justify the author's opinion, and do not find it necessary to add but few special notes to the body of this work, in order to show that it fails to confirm the late origin of the Pentateuch. The "Introductory on Dr. Kuenen's *Religion of Israel*" examines the validity of these reasons as presented by the Dutch school, and I do not wish to enlarge this work by a mere repetition of the argument in another form and in other words. The same may be said of the special arguments of Graf and several other writers.

This work is not addressed to scholars, but is an appeal to the sound sense and sober thought of the people. It has been published at the request, however, of scholars, professors in theological schools, and ministers of different denominations, for their own use and for the use of their classes and parishes. I have not, therefore, filled the bottom of the page with references, as it would have been very easy to have done; for they would have been utterly useless to the great body of the people, for whose instruction I send forth this book. Let my readers take their Bibles and compare my argument in this "Study," as they read it, with the sacred narrative, and exercise the same sound, practical judgment respecting its validity which they exercise in the common affairs of life, and I have no fear of the result. May the Source of all Truth bless this endeavor to find and proclaim it!

I have in manuscript, ready for the press, a "Popular Introduction, or Common-Sense View of the Books of the Old Testament," which I hope in good time to publish.

RUFUS P. STEBBINS.

NEWTON CENTRE, MASS., October, 1881.

ERRATA.

Several errors, principally verbal and grammatical, in this volume, will be corrected in future editions. The following errors of most importance are here corrected: —

Page 11, thirteenth line, for "he" read "earlier writers"; fourteenth line, for "his" read "their." In foot-note on same page, for "38" read "24."

Page 29, fifth line, instead of "None is given,— not a line, not a letter," read "Some proof of a part of them, very weak and inconclusive, is attempted, Vol. I., page 283 and following."

Page 33, first line of note, after "by" read "or after the time of."

Page 134, section iv., seventh line, omit "Joshua and."

Page 152, fourth line from bottom, insert "some of" after "by," and after "Leviticus" insert "xvii.—"

Page 175, note, fifth line, for "442, 443," read "432, 433."

Page 193, eleventh line from the bottom, read "sufficient" for "insufficient."

Page 196, fourth line, for "xxix." read "xxviii."

CONTENTS.

PAGE

INTRODUCTORY ON "KUENEN'S RELIGION OF ISRAEL," 7
A STUDY OF THE PENTATEUCH.
    I. INTRODUCTION, ... 75
    II. EXTERNAL EVIDENCES, ... 82
    III. INTERNAL EVIDENCES, ... 157
ANALYTICAL INDEX, ... 231

INTRODUCTORY

ON

Dr. KUENEN'S "RELIGION OF ISRAEL." *

OF the brilliant constellation of Dutch Biblical critics which has just risen above the horizon, Dr. Kuenen appears to be the principal star. His works on *The Religion of Israel* and *The Prophets and Prophecy in Israel* are by far the most extensive and elaborate of any works of this new and able school of writers. The eyes of scholars are now turned from Germany to Holland; and the wonder of some and the admiration of others are challenged to the utmost. Condemnation and laudation will be visited upon these authors in unstinted measure; for they give no quarter to dissentients, and will, therefore, receive none from them. They write in a tone of perfect self-reliance, and hold in low estimate any opinions not corresponding with theirs. The infallibility of the late Pio Nono was modesty compared with the dogmatic certainty with which they make affirmations upon subjects about

---

* *The Religion of Israel to the Fall of the Jewish State.* By Dr. A. Kuenen, Professor of Theology at the University of Leyden. Translated from the Dutch by Alfred Heath May. Vol. I., pp. ix., 412. 1874. Vol. II., pp. 307. 1875. Vol. III., pp. 345. 1875. 8vo. Williams & Norgate, 14 Henrietta Street, Covent Garden, London, and 20 South Frederick Street, Edinburgh.

which such scholars as Gesenius, Ewald, De Wette, to say nothing of others hardly their inferiors, hesitated to give an opinion, much less to dogmatize. The emphatic manner in which they announce as finalities some of the flimsiest of their speculations and hypotheses provokes a smile.* There will be ample and frequent opportunity to illustrate this signal characteristic of the work under review in the course of this essay.

The style of this work of Dr. Kuenen's is as dry as it is dogmatic. We are informed, by those competent to judge, that the translator has done no injustice to the original. It is true that freshness and raciness are not to be expected as the prime qualities of a work of this kind; yet it ought to be exempt from jejuneness, and to be animated and warm with the dignity and importance of the subject. It should surely kindle some enthusiasm to trace the history of a people like the Jews, and describe a literature which includes such writings as the Book of Job, the Psalms, and the prophecies of Isaiah and Amos and Joel and Hosea. It is true that Dr. Kuenen is not writing a history of the literature of Israel, and may not have felt any of the admiration which an appreciative reader of these marvellous productions cannot suppress, as he feels the glow and heart-throb in every syllable of the ancient poet. His eye was fixed almost exclusively on "altars" and "asheras" and "bull-gods," and "chiuns" and "chemoshes" and "Molochs" and "Levites" and "priests" and the "ritual" that was not before Ezekiel "certainly," not before Ezra "probably." Dr. Kuenen's theme was the "religion," not

* See Appendix A, p. 59.

the literature, of Israel, and he is not to be blamed but praised for adhering to it. If it was a dry subject, it was not his fault. He is responsible only for its treatment. To an examination of this, we will now address ourselves.

Dr. Kuenen, in the three octavo volumes before us, treats of the development of the "Religion of Israel" from the earliest period down "to the fall of the Jewish State." He does not fail of doing justice to the theme for want of space. Three octavo volumes, including over one thousand closely-printed pages, cannot be judged a cramped or an abbreviated discussion of the subject. As far as quantity is concerned, there is no ground for fault-finding. What, then, is the *quality* of the work done by the author?

With an honorable frankness, at the very start Dr. Kuenen states his "stand-point," his "sources of information," and "the plan and division" of his history. "Our stand-point," he says, "is sketched in a single stroke, as it were, by the manner in which this work sees the light. It does not stand entirely alone, but is one of a number of monographs on 'the principal religions.' For us, the Israelitish is one of these religions, nothing less, but also nothing more." These religions may differ from each other in value, but one is no more a special revelation from God than another. Christianity belongs in the same category. All religions claim to be revelations from God, and the claims of all are equally delusive. This is the author's "stand-point," from which he views and discusses the "religion of Israel."* It is not our purpose to chal-

* Vol. I., pp. 5-12.

lenge its justness, at least not in this stage of the discussion.

The author's "sources of information" are "the entire literature of Israel, so far as it originated in the period" of which he treats. The value of each writer's opinion and testimony must be determined by the age in which he lived and the authorities which he used. Hence "it is of the highest importance to trace out and determine, first of all, the age of the various books and of their several constituent parts,— for instance, of the different prophets and psalms." But the authors of the historical books of the Old Testament, from Genesis to Esther, were not contemporaries with the events which they record; and, therefore, we cannot receive their account of the origin and development of their religion, *unless it agrees with the laws of human progress*, as understood by the author. These histories also contain narratives of incredible events, miracles,— such as the passage of the Red Sea and the Jordan, the manna, the wandering in the wilderness, the giving of the law at Sinai. All these events are simply impossible, and are therefore incredible. Hence, we discover that these writers "fearlessly allowed themselves to be guided in their statements by the wants of the present and the requirements of the future. They considered themselves exempt from all responsibility." The priests and the prophets took opposite views, and perverted history to sustain their respective opinions. The narrative of the same transaction in the Books of the Kings differs widely from that given in the Books of the Chronicles. In these latter and later books, the priests colored or invented the history to suit their ends, without regard to truth.*

We give an illustration referred to by Dr. Kuenen as a type of the style of these falsifying historians: "If any one wishes to form an idea of the modifications which the materials supplied by *tradition* underwent upon being worked up afresh, let him compare together II. Kings xi., and II. Chronicles xxii., 10;—xxiii., 21. If the chronicler, under the influence of his sympathy for priests and Levites, could give such an *entirely different version* of the elevation of Joash to the throne of his fathers, which was related with perfect clearness in the older account, with which he was well acquainted, how much more likely" was it that he should handle the more ancient narratives in a manner to answer his *priestly* end. (The italics are ours.)

Such is the statement of Dr. Kuenen's chosen illustration of the partisan bias of the chronicler, and its influence on his work. Let us examine its value and by it judge the value of all such accusations.

I. Dr. Kuenen says his "materials were supplied by *tradition.*" The chronicler says that these things and more "are *written* in the story of the Book of the Kings," xxiv., 27; and the historian of the reign of Joash, in II. Kings xi., xii., says that "the rest of the acts of Joash and all that he did are *written* . . . in the Book of the Chronicles of the kings of Judah." Both writers relied upon written documents and *not* upon "tradition." Comment is unnecessary.

II. Dr. Kuenen assumes that the chronicler had before him no written documents except our Book of Kings, and that he "worked up" the facts there re-

* Vol. I., p. 38.

corded as he pleased. The work which he refers to here and in other places is apparently a very different one from our Book of Kings, and was undoubtedly the public records which had been saved during the captivity. But how could Dr. Kuenen say that his "materials were supplied by tradition," when he was perfectly "well acquainted" with the "older account" in Kings, which he had "worked up" to suit his priestly ends?

III. Dr. Kuenen accuses the writer of falsifying history to sustain the priestly pretensions, not to say usurpations, of his age, for two reasons : one, because he is fuller in his account of the action of the priests during the reign of Joash, and the other, apparently, because, if the chronicler's narrative is substantially correct, his, Dr. Kuenen's, theory of the development of the religion of Israel is false. We have nothing to say about the latter reason. Of the former, we say that the writer of the Kings may be in error. But there is no reason to suppose that both writers are not substantially correct. There is no direct contradiction between them. Applying the common rule of criticism, that "what one does by another he does himself," there is no appearance of contradiction in their accounts. Jehoiada, the high-priest, and the priests, are represented in Kings as being very active in both civil and religious affairs. The special services which they rendered in both are more fully narrated by the chronicler ; but there is not a shadow of evidence that he was laboring under such an ecclesiastical bias as to lead him to falsify history, that he might exalt the priesthood to honor. On the contrary, he relates, without rebuke, how, in the great reformation under Hezekiah, II. Chronicles xxix., 34, when "the priests were too few, so that they could not flay all the burnt offerings, their brethren, the Levites, did help them till the work was ended, and until the other priests had sanctified themselves; *for the Levites were more upright in heart to sanctify themselves than the priests.*" A writer whose purpose was to elevate the priesthood above the Levites would not have thus written. See also xxx., 15, 17; xxxv., 10–15.

IV. Dr. Kuenen says the chronicler gives "an entirely different version of the elevation of Joash to the throne" from the writer of Kings. Let us note the facts: Jehosheba "took Joash and hid him and his nurse in the bed-chamber from Athaliah, so that he was not slain" in the massacre of the rest of the family; so also the chronicler states. He was hid six years; so the chronicler. And in the seventh year Jehoiada gathered the rulers over hundreds and other officers into the house of the Lord, where they took an oath and made a covenant, and showed them the king's son and crowned him, stationing a guard in different parts of the city and temple; the chronicler only adds that in the temple as guards none but priests and Levites entered. When Athaliah learned what was done, and cried "Treason!" she was slain; so the chronicler. And Jehoiada took the king to the king's house, and sat him on the throne of the kingdom: the same in Chronicles, save that Jehoiada arraigned also the priests, that the services of the temple might be renewed, as it is "written in the law of Moses." Are these "*entirely* different versions of the elevation of Joash to the throne of his fathers"? We submit that it would be difficult to find two accounts of the coronation of Queen Victoria more alike. We are curious to know what accounts Dr. Kuenen would call similar if these are *"entirely different."* *

But it is time to return from specific criticism to a consideration of the main course of argument in the work before us; were we to yield to the temptation offered, we should write a volume.

Such being "the condition of the sources of our information," Dr. Kuenen may well ask, "How are we to endeavor to arrive at historical truth" respecting the religion of the people?

The answer to this question discloses the *"plan"* of the author. It is as follows:—

"We offer, for instance, a supposition with respect to the Mosaic period. On the strength of various indications, we assume that the people of Israel and the man who delivered them out of their bondage in Egypt had reached such and such a degree of religious development. We proceed with our investigation, and gradually come to the centuries during which the narratives about Moses and his work were written down. We now succeed in showing that, "*if our conception of the course of historical development be the true one*, the representation given in these narratives must *necessarily have been formed at that time,* and could have assumed no other shape."†

This is frank and intelligible. The author informs us that he "*assumes*" as an historical verity a certain state of "religious development," and then affirms that if, according to *his* theory of the evolution of ideas and human progress, the condition of the people, five or ten

* Vol. I., pp. 12-27.   † Vol. I., pp. 26-32.

centuries later, conforms to the demands of the theory, the "assumed" state of things was correct, and the representation of those early ages given in the historical books must have been merely the *mistaken conception of the writers;* and proves that all narratives containing such representations of opinions must have been written at a later period, since no such opinions, according to his theory of development, could have been entertained by the men of the Mosaic age, nor long subsequent to it. In short, Dr. Kuenen has a theory respecting what could, and could not, have been believed and done in the Mosaic and following age; *and since the historical books do not sustain that theory, they are not ancient, they are not reliable;* the writers have attributed opinions, laws, customs of their own times to the time of their great ancestor. It does not appear to have occurred to Dr. Kuenen that his theory may be wrong, and that the old histories may be substantially correct. Now if his theory, or assumption, or "supposition" is without solid foundation in reason and undoubted facts, then the whole elaborate structure of his work,—

> "Like the baseless fabric of a vision,
> ... shall dissolve,
> And leave not a rack behind."

Such is the "*plan*," the theory, which is to determine the age and value of the Old Testament books and the opinions which were prevalent among the Israelites in the time of Moses, and in all subsequent times:—if a book contains opinions and describes customs and alludes to religious rites, which, *according to Dr. Kuenen's theory, could not have been developed and prevalent at so early a period, then the writer, unwittingly or maliciously, states what is false; for all historical truth or falsehood is to be tested by this theory.* It is the Procrustean bed on which all statements are to be fitted, however great the compression or extension.

Where, then, does the author think he finds solid ground on which he may stand, and whence he can take his departure and apply his theory of historical verity? As there is almost no historical literature extant which was composed before the captivity, 588 B.C., the writings of the early prophets are examined to learn the condition of religion and religious customs in Israel, 808–700 B.C. Amos, Hosea, Isaiah, Zechariah, Micah, and Nahum are accepted as authority, and quoted to show what opinions were prevalent, and what rites were customary in the eighth century before Christ, the fifth or sixth century after Moses. Dr. Kuenen does not omit the prophet Joel on any theoretical grounds, but because some writers place him in a later period. There is no valid reason, however, why the writings of Joel, as well as those of the other prophets named, should not be considered as good authority for the religious condition of this period.

In order to understand the bearing of these quotations on Dr. Kuenen's theory, it is necessary now to state, in as intelligible a manner as brevity will admit, the order of the evolution of religious ideas, as *assumed* in this theory among men, and especially among the ancestors of the Israelites, and among the Israelites themselves. The first religious state is fetichism, pre-Abrahamic; then polytheism, sub-Abrahamic, down to the return from the captivity; then monotheism. A few men were monotheists so far as Israel was concerned. This people had but one God. They believed, however, there were other gods for other nations, and no more doubted their existence than they doubted the existence of Jahveh. Moses was one of these, and others succeeded him; but they were few who believed in but one God for Israel. The idea of God became purer, however, as generations passed away, till, in the eighth century, in the time of Amos, very much more worthy and nobler views were entertained of the nature and character of the Supreme Being, and worthier and purer worship was demanded. The sacrifices of beasts and fruits were remanded to a secondary place, and human sacrifices were pronounced abhorrent to God. Moses wrote nothing of the Pentateuch but an abbreviated form of the Ten Commandments or "Ten Words." A few chapters in Exodus and Leviticus may have been composed before settling in Canaan; but the Book of Deuteronomy was not composed till the reign of Josiah, 620 B.C., and the historical portions of the four other books were not written till the captivity. Ezra and his fellow-priests drew up nearly the whole ritual as we now find it in Leviticus and the other books of the Pentateuch just before his return to Jerusalem from Babylon, and brought it with him, and introduced it, with the aid of Nehemiah and the priests, as a Mosaic production, and venerable with age and the observance of the fathers; and the Books of Chronicles were written, perverting and falsifying history, to sustain the false claim of Ezra's ritual to antiquity and the supremacy of the tribe of Levi, and the dignity and sacredness of the priesthood. The older historian of the Books of the Kings had no knowledge of any such ritual and priesthood. The prophets disappeared before the new order of priests, and the voice of the poet-preacher was stifled by the smoke of holocausts.

In due time, after centuries of struggle, suffering, despair, and hope, the great Teacher came and announced a spiritual worship, demanding no sacrifice but a devout heart, no temple but a consecrated spirit; and Judaism blossomed into Christianity, and the religion of Israel was transformed into the religion of the world. Such is substantially Dr. Kuenen's theory of the development of religious ideas in Israel, and the origin of the books of the Old Testament. We are confident that we have not omitted any important particular or element of it.

We now return to an examination of Dr. Kuenen's method of laying the foundation of his proof of this theory or hypothesis in the writings of the prophets, named on a previous page, who wrote during the eighth century before Christ, or five or six centuries after the putative time of Moses. And now let it be most distinctly understood that the historical books are ruled out of this discussion for the present by Dr. Kuenen's own decision of their modern date and careless or unscrupulous writers. He must not refer to them when they record something which corresponds with his theory, and ignore them or challenge them when they record something which opposes his theory. No doubt he intends to hold the scales evenly balanced, but he is sometimes tempted beyond what he is able to bear to appeal as authority to the very witness he has pronounced not trustworthy. Examples of this weakness would be given were it necessary for our purpose, but our space is all of it to the last letter demanded for our special object, namely, to show *the radical defect and failure* of Dr. Kuenen's supposed proof of his theory respecting the origin of these books, and hence of the origin and development of the "Religion of Israel."

In the very brief writings of these prophets, "monotheism" is most emphatically taught, and the sin of worshipping idols and serving the gods of other nations is most emphatically rebuked; and the severest calamities are threatened if they forsake "the law of" Jehovah; and "captivity" as well as "drouth" and "locusts" are predicted as the portion of the nation, if the people obey not God, and do not observe his "commandments." The temple was in existence, sacrifices were offered, feasts were kept, "priests" served at the altar, and "the law" was often appealed to as a rule of duty. In these brief fragments of the poetic addresses of the prophets, we have allusions to all the main features of the ritual service as described in Chronicles and Ezra. The sternness of the rebukes of these prophets, when they saw the wickedness of the people in making and worshipping idols, is not strange; is far from being "a remarkable phenomenon," even when producing open "conflict" and persecution. What may be done and said without opposition in Holland now we do not know; but what was done to free speakers and writers centuries ago we know well enough; and we know that in later times Fox and Wesley and Whitefield were persecuted as bitterly as those prophets of 800 B.C., to say nothing of Rogers and Cranmer, the martyrs of bloody Mary, and the victims of the merciless Jeffries, cruelly tortured in the blasphemed name of religion. There are no "causes" far to seek, or hard to understand, as Dr. Kuenen supposes, why these prophets were assailed by the law-breakers, the cruel, the false, the idol-worshippers, and idol-makers. The "conflict" is as old as time, and will continue till time shall be no longer. Yet our author infers — nay, affirms — that this "conflict" and persecution could not have arisen if the Pentateuch had existed.

One would suppose that Dr. Kuenen would now examine with closest scrutiny these statements, so clear and explicit, and their bearing upon his theory, which these writers, whose veracity he does not question, furnish so abundantly. He does no such thing. He hastens to inquire into "the earlier fortune of the people of Israel," as if he perceived that these prophets furnished his theory no support. But what materials has he, on his own theory, to furnish him any information about it? Not a line of history was written, as he affirms, till this period, or later; and what was written then was "not historical." The writers of most of these historical books, called so only by way of courtesy, lived, on the theory of Dr. Kuenen, after these prophets, and "considered themselves exempt from all responsibility" as to the truth of the events which they narrate. If there is no reliable record of events previous to 800 B.C., we are very much at a loss to guess where he gets his information. If he writes from his "inner consciousness" only, his history has no more reliable source than that of those old Jewish writers whom he so soundly berates for their groundless stories. If the Books of the Kings and of Samuel are not reliable accounts, how can he quote them as he does to show the state, civil and religious, of the people "earlier" than the eighth century? We stand firmly here. Dr. Kuenen must either reject or accept these historical books as being substantially reliable. If he accepts them, then the controversy is ended, and his emphatic condemnation of the untrustworthiness of their writers is a gross injustice. If he rejects them, then he has no right to appeal to them as authority in any case whatever. He can take which horn of the dilemma he chooses. He cannot be permitted to select here and there a story, cull out here and there a sentence, because it answers the purposes of his theory and confirms his "assumption," and reject all the rest.

The references to the early history and customs of the people from the time of Abraham onward are so numerous in these prophets that Dr. Kuenen confesses that we should be compelled to suppose that at least Micah "was acquainted with those narratives" as contained in the Pentateuch, "unless appearances should tend to show that they were written or modified at a later date,"— that is, later than the time of these prophets;* and this Dr. Kuenen believes. They were *not* written till the time of the captivity, or two hundred years later than the time of these prophets. What these prophets say, therefore, about the early past, they have no authority for. They only express "*the idea which was entertained of that history in the eighth century*

* Vol. I., pp. 102, 103.

B.C." Be it so. Then it is only repeating the folly of the "wild ass that eateth up the east wind" to rake over the stories in Genesis and Exodus, which were not committed to writing till two centuries after this period, to supplement the "ideas" of the eighth century as given by these prophets. Our author does it, however, and concludes that Abraham, Isaac, and Jacob "*are not historical personages.*" Nor are the twelve tribes descendants of Jacob's twelve sons. There may be some truth, but not much, in the account of the emigration from Egypt, the wandering in the wilderness, the entrance and partial conquest of Canaan, and the anarchical condition from the time of Joshua to the coronation of Saul. But he who believes least of what is told is the wisest man.*

Dr. Kuenen, however, becomes so enamoured with these old story-tellers that he gives us three chapters more upon "The Israelitish Prophets before and during the Eighth Century B.C.," and "The Course of Israel's Religious Development," and "The History of Israel's Religious Development before and during the Eighth Century B.C." Now let it be most distinctly understood that for every fact, or supposed fact, in these three chapters, covering two hundred and twenty-four pages, Dr. Kuenen is indebted to these same books which he affirms to have been written not only by men who lived from a thousand to five hundred years after the events described, but by men who "considered themselves exempted from all responsibility" to tell the truth! No statement of fantastic act in the life of Samson would be antecedently more incredible than

* Vol. I., p. 384.

this. And yet the thing has been done by a renowned scholar,— the pages are open before us in all their compact beauty. But if Dr. Kuenen's theory is correct, if his statements respecting the unhistorical character of these books are to be accepted, then it is the beauty of a harlot; for he can put no more historical truth into these chapters of *his* book than he finds in these books of the Old Bible; and, if they are untrue, these chapters are untrue. The same fountain cannot send forth sweet waters and bitter, truth and lies. The logic of the whole matter is, that methods and places of worship, customs and habits of life, prevailed, according to these writers, down to this eighth century, in direct violation of the Mosaic law as recorded in the Pentateuch, and which would *not* have prevailed had the Mosaic law been in existence or been known by the people. *Therefore*, the Mosaic laws, so called, were not composed till after the eighth century B.C.! A most magnificent *non sequitur*. As if the violation of a law was any evidence that the law was not on the statute-book! Or, to state the matter differently, as if the performance of an act was proof that there was no law against it, or that the existence of a custom was proof that there was no statute forbidding it. According to these "unhistorical" books of unknown authorship and irresponsible composition, other men than priests offered sacrifices, in other places than at the tabernacle. Punishments were inflicted by men having no authority, and which were cruel and vindictive to the last degree. The laws of Moses, in a word, were not observed, and *therefore* they did not exist,— one of the most inconclusive inferences which could possibly be drawn. All history shows its fallacy.*

Passing on from the eighth century B.C., the next chapter treats of "The Religion of Israel to the Fall of Jerusalem, in B.C. 588." The only two points of special interest discussed in this chapter are (1) the reform under Hezekiah, who overthrew the altars of the idols, and cut down the groves [or the asheras], and made a very thorough change in the administration of the religion of the people; and (2) the finding of the "Book of the Law," in the reign of Josiah, by Hilkiah, the priest. It is necessary to pause a moment to consider the value of these incidents in settling the age of the Pentateuch.

Hezekiah attempted to reform the worship of the people, which, it is very important to note, for over a century had been growing grosser and grosser, like the ceremonies of the Romish Church during the Dark Ages. Idols were set up and altars erected and sacrifices offered on the "high places." The prophets denounced these practices in vain. The kings were satisfied to administer the civil law; and on grounds of

* It is objected repeatedly by other writers that the absence of the record of any enforcement of a law is sufficient proof that no such law existed. See *Unitarian Review*, October 1880, p. 300, *passim*. "Good kings did not remove idolatrous worship," therefore there was no law against idolatry. How much these good kings did toward ridding the kingdom of idolatry we do not know. That they did not *wholly* succeed is all that can be inferred from the passage Can it not be said that we had good governors who did not shut up the liquor-shops, and good mayors who did not close the most popular gambling saloons? Does it follow that there was no prohibitory law in Boston, because there were more than two thousand bars where liquor was sold? We know there was. There are also hundreds of vile houses in Boston which the good mayor has not shut up. Is there no law against them? Such reasoning would not be tolerated in the lowest form of a grammar school.

expediency, or supposing, by some method of interpretation of their own, that idol-worship was consistent with the worship of Jehovah, they not only permitted but encouraged it, as the popes encouraged image-worship and the selling of indulgences. The nation had departed no further from the requirements of the Mosaic law — assuming that it was given as early as his time — than the Church of the sixth to the tenth centuries had departed from the teachings of Christ. But customs are not easily changed; and, though Hezekiah appears to have been in earnest, he could not eradicate the religious rites and opinions which had been cherished and firmly rooted with increasing vigor for more than three generations. He did his best to purify their worship; but, when he died, reaction came, and a return to the long established and cherished customs. For two generations, or during the long reign of Manasseh, of fifty-five years, and the brief reign of Amon, of two years, idolatry was practised in its worst forms. The restraint under Hezekiah gave way to unbridled license under Manasseh, as the restraint of the Commonwealth gave way to the license of Charles II. and James II. He not only re-erected the "high places," but he "built altars in the house of the LORD, . . . and he built altars for all the hosts of heaven, in the two courts of the house of the LORD. And he made his son pass through fire, and observed times and used enchantments and dealt with familiar spirits and wizards." He set one of the abominable "graven images of the grove," as our translation names it to conceal its obscenity, "in the house of the Lord," in the very temple itself, — a baseness of profanation of which even Athaliah did not dream or Ahaz attempt. *They* appear to have reverently closed the temple doors, and to have erected their idols only in the courts. Nor is this all. "Moreover, Manasseh shed innocent blood very much, till he had filled Jerusalem, from one end to the other." What horrors of martyrdom the reformers under Hezekiah suffered, these few words but dimly hint. The true prophets fled and concealed themselves, or were slaughtered. The true priests escaped as they could, and suffered all extremities, even to perishing with hunger. The reaction and persecution under Mary Tudor were not greater or bloodier or more merciless than those under Manasseh. And this prevalence of idolatry continued for seventy-five years, till Josiah again attempted a reform; and this persecution of Hezekiah's reformers continued till the last voice was silenced and the last hand cold.

Nothing in Dr. Kuenen's work has so awakened our regret, not to say our indignation in this instance, as his attempt to palliate the abominations and atrocities of Manasseh, saying that he "represented a conviction" as well as Hezekiah. The "account [of his cruelties] is unworthy of credit," affirms Dr. Kuenen. He only did what his grandfather Ahaz did in setting up idols, and causing his son to pass through fire! "Free from all exclusivism, Manasseh cannot well have become a persecutor of his own accord. If he took this part upon him, he was driven to it by the reception accorded to his measures!" No doubt. Mary Tudor's measures were not accepted; and, lo, the stake, the rack, the red-hot iron! Isabella's measures were not received; and, lo, the horrors of the Inquisition! We have read apologies for Judas Iscariot with considerable patience; for the poor fellow saw his guilt and shame, and hung himself. But we have no hint that Manasseh ever relented in his work of blood, or was abashed in the presence of his "groves," or "asheras." He persecuted as long as a hunted victim could be found. He practised his licentious rites as long as subjects for their lustful orgies could be furnished. He stands eminent among the Anakims of cruelty, though he had "a conviction," as Mary Tudor had, as James II. had, as Torquemada had,—"*a conviction*"! Heaven help us to escape "convictions"!

We now turn to consider the origin, character, and extent of the reform under Josiah. For personal reasons, probably, Amon, the son of Manasseh, after a brief reign of two years, was assassinated by his servants in his own house. The people punished the assassins, and placed his son Josiah, only eight years of age, on the throne. Under influences which are not named, his counsellors appear to have administered civil affairs wisely, without interfering with the forms of religion, till, in the eighteenth year of his reign, while the temple was undergoing repairs, Hilkiah, the high-priest, informs Shaphan, the scribe, that he had "*found the book of the law in the house of the* LORD." It was read before the King, and he was so moved in view of the sins of the people, as revealed by this "book of the law," that "he rent his clothes," and directed that measures should be taken at once to obey "the book of the law." He gathered the elders of the people, and "the book" was read in their hearing, even "all the words of the book of the covenant." Then the King and the people "made a covenant before the LORD to walk after the LORD, and to keep his commandments and his testimonies and his statutes with all their heart and all their soul, and to perform the words of this covenant that were written in this book." The work commences of conforming to the law as recorded in this book. "The high-priest and priests of the second order" bring out of the temple all the vessels of Baal, and the shameful ashera, "grove," burn them, and carry the ashes to Bethel. He displaced the "idolatrous priests who burned incense in the high places unto Baal, to the sun and to the moon and to the planets and to all the host of heaven. He brake down the houses of the Sodomites, that were by the house of the LORD, and defiled the high places and Topheth." He burned to ashes all that would burn, and ground to powder all that could be pulverized, of the articles used in idol-worship; and, having cleansed the land of idolatry, he commanded the passover to be kept as directed "in the book of this covenant." But it was too late. Josiah was killed in a battle with Pharaoh-Nechoh; and under his sons the nation again relapsed into idolatry, and Jerusalem was taken, and the captivity followed.

Now, what was this "*book of the law of the Lord*" which aroused Josiah to attempt a radical reform in the religious practices of the nation? Dr. Kuenen says: "Moses bequeathed no book of the law to the tribes of Israel. Certainly, nothing more was committed to writing by him, or in his time, than 'the ten words,'" the ten commandments, "in their original form." How, we ask with significant emphasis, how does Dr. Kuenen know that Moses wrote these "ten words"? or that they were written as early as his day? Where is the proof of it? None is given,—not a line, not a letter. The testimony of the "inner consciousness" cannot be taken in this case; and we challenge him to bring any proof that Moses wrote "the ten words" which will not also prove that he wrote a great many words.* Dr. Kuenen says that the fragmentary laws in existence before Josiah's time would not satisfy what he calls the "Mosaic party,"— that is, the anti-idolatrous portion of the people,— and some one or more of them, Hilkiah or others, forged "a book of the law of the Lord," in the name of the old lawgiver. "Notions about literary property were then in their infancy." They would have no "qualms of conscience" who declared they had "found" a book when they did not find it, but wrote it; nor when they attributed its authorship to Moses, *though they knew they lied!* The Mosaic party must gain their end at all hazards. "Now or never,"— hence forgery and lying are justifiable. That forgery — as unblushing and more criminal than the forged election returns in Louisiana,

---

* A writer in the *Unitarian Review*, November, 1880, pp. 435, 436, says the ten commandments, as written on the tablets of stone, are not given in the second writing, Exodus xxxiv., as in the first, Exodus xx. The historian says they were. Compare Exodus xxxiv., 1, and xxxiv., 27, 28. The writer mistakes when he understands that the laws given in this chapter were written on the two tables. They were written as the other laws were. Moses was commanded to write these words or commands because they were "*after the tenor*," based upon the words or commands *given before*. There were not ten of them, no more, no less; but a code of rules based upon the ten laws or commandments, which were written on the tables, and not here repeated. They are not said *to be the words* of the covenant, but "*after the tenor*," based upon them.

or the Decretals — was the Book of Deuteronomy; not the whole of it, but Deuteronomy iv., 44 — xxvi. and xxviii. These chapters, no more, no less, were deliberately forged for a religious purpose at this time. Now, what is the proof of it? Let us pick up as we may the alleged evidence produced by Dr. Kuenen.

1. "The first four books of the Pentateuch are more recent than the seventh century before our era"; and therefore they cannot be, either one or all of them, the book "found" or forged, the latter, not the former, in Josiah's reign. But this is simply taking for granted what must be proved. No evidence, not a line, has yet been brought by Dr. Kuenen to show that the first four books of the Pentateuch were not written till after this period, save that laws contained in it were often violated, and sometimes with impunity.

2. "Let it be further remembered that the writing found by Hilkiah is called the '*book of the law*,' and the '*book of the covenant*.'" It is true that in Deuteronomy iv., 44, we read, "And this is the law which Moses set before the children of Israel. These are the testimonies and statutes and judgments which Moses spake unto the children of Israel." And in chapter v., 2, 3, it is said that "the Lord our God made a covenant with us in Horeb." But in no place is Deuteronomy called "the book of the law," or "the book of the covenant." But we read in Exodus xxiv., 7, that Moses took *the book of the covenant*, and read in the audience of the people; and numerous sections of the other books of the Pentateuch are called "the law." The inference drawn by Dr. Kuenen, from the possible meaning of the phrases "the law" and "the

covenant," as used in Deuteronomy, is therefore not valid, and is far from proving that only the last book of the Pentateuch is referred to, excluding the others.

3. "It cannot have been of any great length, if we may believe the statement that it was read by Shaphan, and then read before Josiah in one day." This would be true of any of the sections named "*the law*" and "the covenant," which are contained in any of the books. These important sections might all be read more easily than twenty-three chapters in Deuteronomy. The only possible objection to this view is found in one word in the history of this transaction, II. Kings xxiii., 2 : "And he read in their ears *all* the words of the book of the covenant,"— as if the whole of the book, whatever the topic, was read. There are large sections of Deuteronomy which have no special relation to the reforms instituted by Josiah ; and laws respecting all his reforms are found in other portions of the Pentateuch. Certainly, Dr. Kuenen will not rest the proof that "*the book of the law*" read before Josiah was our present Book of Deuteronomy, on the single use of the word " all " by a historian who is not known, and who belongs to a class of writers who are said by himself "to consider themselves exempt from all responsibility" to write the truth. We however believe this writer was honest, and intended to tell the truth, and did tell it ; and that what he said is that " all " was read which pertained to the Being whom they worshipped, and the place and form of worship then necessary to be known, and the penalties which would follow disregard of this law.

4. The final reason given by Dr. Kuenen for believ-

ing that Deuteronomy is "the book of the law" found, forged, by Hilkiah is that the customs reformed are all rebuked in Deuteronomy, and the penalties threatened for transgression are there written. But all these threatenings and all these laws are also contained in other books of the Pentateuch. It is not necessary, therefore, to infer that the reading would be confined to the last of the five books. Hilkiah or Shaphan may have made selections from any part of "the book of the law" which were appropriate to the occasion. What book this was which Hilkiah "found" or forged must be determined in a very different manner from that which Dr. Kuenen has adopted. In the proper place, we shall give it the consideration which it demands.

The seventh chapter on "The Israelitish Exiles in Babylon" contains so little which bears upon the question which we are discussing that we shall pass it by with the single remark that it is very full and able, giving a correct view of the condition of the exiles, and the influences of the peoples among whom they dwelt upon their religious ideas and forms.

The eighth chapter, which describes the return from the captivity and "The Establishment of the Hierarchy and the Introduction of the Law," demands special attention; for we are here told of the origin of the rest of the Pentateuch, and especially of the composition and introduction of the ritual law. As the subject is a large one, and our space is limited, we must confine ourselves to those points which have direct reference to the origin of the Pentateuch and the historical books.

Dr. Kuenen affirms in the strongest language * that "the priestly laws" and "priestly ordinances were made known and imposed upon the Jewish nation *now for the first time*," by Ezra, 457 B.C. "They were not laws which had been long in existence, and which were now proclaimed afresh and accepted by the people, after having been forgotten for a while. *No written ritual legislation existed in Ezekiel's time.*" † During the first thirteen years after Ezra's return, he perfected the code which he had brought with him from Babylon, *where he and others drew it up*. It received some modifications at the hand of Nehemiah, and perhaps others; and this code of laws was palmed off upon the returned exiles as "*God's law which was given by* ['the hand of'] *Moses, the servant of God*," and which they bound themselves by a solemn oath, under a curse, to obey (Nehemiah x., 29). No priest discovered the fraud; no scribe, versed in the traditions, customs, and laws of the nation, had a suspicion that this formidable, exacting, and onerous code was a barefaced forgery, a prodigious fraud; or else they were all silent in the very face of an imposition upon the credulity of a long-suffering nation, without a parallel in the history of the

---

* Vol II., p. 230.

† Dr. Kuenen maintains that Leviticus xviii.-xxvi. was written by Ezekiel. There is not a shadow of evidence of it. The peculiar archaisms which are characteristic of the rest of the book and of all the Pentateuch are found in this section, which are not found in the extant writings of Ezekiel, nor in any other writing of the Old Testament subsequent to that of the Pentateuch. He must have taken great pains to imitate the style of the ancient books to conceal this fraud, or some scribe must have tampered with his copy to give it the antique form; and, further, he must have taken great pains in his extant prophecy to refer to this section as containing the laws given to the "fathers," and referring to this forged section as if given in ancient times in the "wilderness" (chapter xx., *passim*), when he knew that he wrote it himself.

world. The stupidity of these people must have been as amazing, as incredible, as was the fraud. There were men and women among these exiles who were not idiots, and who knew whether Ezra was introducing a ritual and law which were new, and not in accordance with the "customs" of the nation before the captivity. There were thousands of those who returned with Zerubbabel from the Babylonian exile, whose fathers had worshipped in the temple which Solomon built, and who were familiar with the whole ritual code. Could their children be blinded to such a degree as not to know a new code so minute in its details, reaching even to the kind and cooking of their food; the material, form, and make of their garments; the construction and care of their houses; the number, amount, and payment of their taxes; the rate of interest and collection of debts; the manner of treating strangers and slaves; the observance of the Sabbath, and the penalty of its desecration? And these are but a few of the laws which touched their persons, their homes, and daily occupations. The bare statement of an hypothesis which demanded such a belief would seem to be its sufficient and swift confutation. Imagine all the men and women and children of those exiles who had refused to sing the songs of their dear native land by the rivers of Babylon, and who had mourned over the loss of their homes, their temple, and their worship, when they had returned to erect anew their altar, and kindle anew its fires, to have had presented for their acceptance such a ritual as they had never heard of; such a religious administration as never before existed in the nation; and yet not a priest, not a Levite, not a scribe, not a prophet, not a prophetess, ever hinted by word or line that this ritual, this code, was new; was not the ritual and code of the fathers; was not the manner of administration and form of worship which prevailed in the land before Jerusalem was destroyed and Judah carried captive! The great company which returned with Zerubbabel had built their homes, and established anew the worship of their nation in the rebuilt temple, and according to the "customs" of the fathers. For over half a century, for *fifty-eight years*, after the dedication of their new temple, "the priests in their divisions, and the Levites in their courses," had conducted the services of the temple, "as it *is written in the book of Moses*"; and twenty years before the temple was finished, on their arrival at Jerusalem, Jeshua and the priests and others "builded an altar to the God of Israel to offer burnt offerings thereon, as *it is written in the law of Moses, the man of God.*" They kept the feast of the tabernacle, "as *it is written*," and "offered the daily burnt offerings by number, according *to the custom.*" They also observed the "new moons, and all the set feasts of the LORD." This large company, with the "high priests" and the "priests" and "Levites" and "singing men" and "singing women" and the "porters" with "the vessels of gold and of silver," and "priests' garments" and "knives," had been keeping "passovers" and "all the feasts," and worshipping according to the "custom" of the fathers, "as written in the book of Moses," "in the law of Moses, the man of God," during two generations, in the undoubting belief that they were honoring God and obeying his law given to their fathers. And yet not a word of astonishment or objection is spoken, no contention arises between these people and the company of Ezra when they return and he introduces his ritual and code which were "*never before heard of*," and " now *for the first time* imposed upon the Jewish nation" ! Every tongue is dumb, every pen is idle; and this unparalleled monstrous forgery is accepted without a word of challenge, a shadow of suspicion, by a people which could boast of such writers as Amos, Isaiah, Micah, Jeremiah, Hosea, Joel, and the Psalmist! If so, the miracles of Egypt, as well as those recorded in the Book of the Judges, become mere commonplace affairs in the history of Israel.

Monstrously incredible as this hypothesis is, Dr. Kuenen has his reasons for adopting it. What are they? It is our duty, as reviewer of his work, to state and examine them. In doing this, we shall be obliged to adopt an order of our own, since Dr. Kuenen's reasons are spread over the whole work, and are interwoven with his whole argument, and are nowhere so arranged in separate paragraphs and distinctly announced as to make verbal quotations easy. We will, however, strive to cover his whole ground with the reasons which we shall name. It will be impossible to refer to the page on which the reasons which we shall state may be found, since they are implied or hinted or assumed through whole chapters, without a brief and clear enunciation. We omit, in this connection, as we shall have occasion to consider it hereafter, the difference in the *style* of the author or authors of the Pentateuch and that of Ezra and the writers of his time, which is to us most conclusive evidence that the Jewish ritual was not the work of any writer who lived after the captivity.*

The first reason which we will notice offered in support of Dr. Kuenen's theory is that *no mention is made* of any such work as the Pentateuch, or any such ritual as it contains, in any work written before the captivity. The value of this reason will depend upon the number and character of the works thus early written. If very few works were written, and they were lyrical like the Psalms, or didactic like the Proverbs, or hortatory like many of the prophets, we should not expect to find formal quotations from the Pentateuch, assuming its early existence, any more than we should expect to find formal quotations from the Gospels in our Christian hymn-books, or in such sermons as Channing's and Robertson's and Bartol's and Martineau's. All that could be expected in such writings would be an occasional allusion, a particular expression, a special phraseology, which would indicate that the writers of these lyric and didactic and prophetic books were familiar with the contents of the Pentateuch, as the sermons of these preachers and the hymns of these poets show that they are familiar with the contents of the Gospels. Whether we do find any such indications of familiarity with the contents of the Pentateuch in the writers before the captivity will be determined subsequently in its proper place.†

But we are by no means willing to confine the testimony to the early origin of the Pentateuch to works written *before* the captivity. What sound reason can

---

* See "Study of the Pentateuch," under "*Style*," page 159 of this volume.
† See "Study of the Pentateuch," under "*Quotations*," page 104 of this volume.

be given for not accepting the testimony of those who wrote after the captivity to events transpiring and customs prevalent before it, if they have good authority for what they say which disappeared soon after, and had in their hands documents which have perished? None whatever. And here we must enter once more our most decided protest against Dr. Kuenen's wholesale accusation and condemnation of the Hebrew writers, historians, and others. There is no evidence that they were shamelessly destitute of veracity, "and considered themselves exempt from all responsibility" to tell the truth, "and fearlessly allowed themselves to be guided in their statements by the wants of the present and the requirements of the future"! After the events of the life of Samuel from 1100 B.C., the writers of Jewish history are exceptionally scrupulous to refer to their authorities. The writer of the Books of the Kings specifies at the close of every section where a full account of what he has very briefly narrated may be found. Bancroft and Palfrey and Parkman are not more scrupulous and frank in informing their readers of the sources of their information. He does not appear to think that he is writing to a set of ignoramuses who could be duped, nor to a party of demagogues who were to be flattered and sustained. Honesty and scholarship glow on every page. If the reader of the Books of the Kings is impressed with any one thing more deeply than another, it is with the truthfulness of the writer. Undoubtedly, he was sometimes mistaken in his interpretation of the old records on which he relied; but not wilfully to gain an end, but humanly as not omniscient. There is no reason to distrust his statements respecting the laws, customs, and religion of the Jews, if he did write four or five hundred years after the reign of David, and closed his history with the fall of Jerusalem and the captivity of Judah; and we shall use his work freely and confidently when we have occasion to do so in this discussion.

We turn now to a consideration of the accuracy and value of the narratives in the Books of the Chronicles. These books are made the subject of the severest criticism by Dr. Kuenen. He accuses the writer of them of very slight regard for truth; of so coloring facts, and of inventing them when there are none, as to sustain the priestly ritual and code forged in the name of Moses by Ezra. Indeed, Dr. Kuenen may be said to believe and maintain that the Books of the Chronicles are substantially historical forgeries composed to give color of truth to the ritual forgeries of Ezra. The priests have invented a religion and forged a history to prove it true.* This all took place, and no scribe of the age, not a man of all the writers of the age, detected the cheat or exposed the falsifier of his nation's history. Mark the point. The writer of the Books of the Chronicles is not a blunderer, an ignorant pretender, an unfortunate bankrupt in authorities: he is an intelligent, deliberate, persistent, and determined falsifier of the annals of his nation which were in his hands; for this writer appeals as constantly to his authorities for his statements as does the writer of the Books of the Kings. Why, then, should Dr. Kuenen assume that where these historians, or rather annalists, differ, the writer of the Chronicles perverts

* Vol. III., p. 70 *et seq.*

or inverts or invents his facts? Why is it impossible that the writer of the Kings may be mistaken? Simply because it would spoil the whole of Dr Kuenen's theory; for it is past all possible question that the priesthood and the ritual are as old as the time of David, if the narratives in the Chronicles are substantially true. But *Carthago delenda est.* The early, especially the Mosaic origin of the priesthood and ritual must be false: *therefore*, every historian asserting its antiquity is thereby shown to be a liar or an ignoramus!

That the writer of the Chronicles is an antiquarian, and often busies himself about very small matters, is true. That he is given to genealogies is also true. That he writes an ecclesiastical and not a civil history is also true. But this does not prove that he deliberately lied, and said that things were as he knew they were not. Neal's *History of the Puritans* differs as much from Hume's history of the same period as the Chronicles differ from the Kings; and yet Neal is as reliable an historian as Hume. He dwells upon other topics and enlarges upon them, and is very diffuse upon some points which Hume omits or only touches. So we find it in the Chronicles. The writer lingers lovingly around topics which the writer of the Kings passes over very lightly or wholly omits, and sometimes they contradict each other. But this is no proof that either of them was a liar. Their authorities may have differed. The figures given in the Chronicles and in the other books are obviously unreliable, for some reason which is not yet explained. The blunders of copyists do not satisfactorily account for all of them. But these obvious mistakes do not affect in the slightest degree the historical accuracy of the statements respecting the religious usages and legal ceremonies of the period of which the work is a fragmentary history,— indeed, only the briefest annals. The fact of a battle having been fought is not discredited because the number of killed and wounded is incorrect, and the name of the commander and the day of the fight are obviously misstated. Genealogies may be erroneous, and yet the events recorded may be substantially correct. It would be a miracle, indeed, if the writer of the Chronicles had made no mistakes in the names of his long lists of ancient families; and a still greater one if the copyists of them for centuries had accurately, letter for letter, reproduced the original. We have tried our hand at both, and do not wish to condemn ourselves by accusing the writer of the Chronicles of being either an idiot or a knave because of the mistakes which are found in his work. There is open before me, as I write, the first volume of Savage's *Genealogy of New England*, a "very miracle of accuracy," and yet there are *twenty octavo pages* of "additions and corrections" at the end of it. How critics of the school of Dr. Kuenen would revel in a volume like this!

After the most patient and long examination of these books, we find nothing which proves or even indicates that their writer falsified his documents and invented incidents. As far as he writes the history of his nation, he writes as a priest would naturally write — religiously. He describes the acts of the priesthood much more fully than those of the civil magistrates. He does not bring his history down further than the destruction of Jerusalem. The books close with the issue of the decree by Cyrus for the return of the captives, 536 B.C. The writer probably composed his work after the return of Nehemiah, and compiled from documents the so-called Books of Ezra and Nehemiah as a fitting appendix to his own work. We submit that there is no valid reason for supposing, with Dr. Kuenen and others, that the Books of Chronicles were not written as early as we have stated, simply because two genealogies of a few names are carried down to 250 B.C. These names might well have been added by a later hand. It may be assumed, therefore, with large measure of assurance, that all the historical books included in our Bible, as we now have them, were composed before 400 B.C., and that they are substantially reliable in their account of the affairs of the nation, both civil and ecclesiastical; that there is no evidence which would be admitted for a moment in any court of justice that these writers were arrant knaves, forging laws and falsifying history; that an indictment based upon such evidence as is adduced against the integrity and ability of these writers would be quashed by any modern court, or a *nol. pros.* would be entered by any prosecuting attorney.

A word must be said respecting the writings which treat of the affairs of the nation from the time of Moses to that of David, a period, according to Dr. Kuenen, of about three hundred years in round numbers,—1300—1000 B.C. The Book of Joshua gives an account of the conquest and division of the land of Canaan among the tribes, and covers a period of about thirty years. If we can rely upon a statement in chap. xvi., 10, "The Canaanites dwell among the Ephraimites [in Gezer] unto this day," the book must have been written before the end of Solomon's reign, for we read, in I. Kings ix., 16, that Pharaoh took Gezer, burned it with fire, slew the Canaanites, and gave it as a present to his daughter, Solomon's wife. This passage would be of little value in overcoming opposing evidence, were there any; but there is none of any weight. The frequent use of the phrase "unto this day" implies some time after the events described, but is very indefinite. This Book of Joshua may have been written as early as the reign of Saul. There is no internal evidence against such a date for its compilation. Its subject is of the conquest, the battles, and the location of the tribes upon their portions of the land. No reasonable critic would expect to find much, if anything, which would treat of their religious manners and customs. What there is said about them we shall call attention to in the proper place.* If there were no allusion to anything of the kind, it would not surprise us, nor should we draw the astounding inference that they were a people without a religion and without a ritual.

The Book of Judges is a very composite work; but if we may rely upon a statement, chap. i., 21, that " the Jebusites dwell with the children of Benjamin in Jerusalem unto this day," the book must have been written before the conclusion of David's reign; for we read in II. Samuel, v., 6–8, that David drove the Jebusites out of Jerusalem, and took the stronghold of Zion, and David dwelt in it. Another passage in one of the appendixes of the book, chap. xviii., 30, may indicate

---

* See "Study of the Pentateuch," under "*Quotations from Joshua*," page 142 of this volume.

that this portion was not written till two or three centuries afterward; for certain persons are said to have served as priests to the tribe of Dan "until the day of the captivity of the land," referring, apparently, to the deportation of the ten tribes of Shalmaneser and Esarhaddon, 721 B.C. As an apology for the lawlessness and insecurity of those days the writer of the appendixes especially calls attention to the fact that there was "no king in Israel in those days" (xviii., 1, and elsewhere). The book was possibly written as illustrative of the importance of a closer union of the tribes and of a stronger central government, or, more probably, it was the work of a curiosity hunter, who gathered the traditions of the most wonderful events which had happened during a period of civil and foreign wars, if border ravages and riotous outbreaks can be called wars, like the feuds of the Scottish clans, or the fights of Miles Standish and Captain Church with the Indians. The writer was an Israelitish Cotton Mather, and his book of the wonders of New England, *Thaumaturgus*, is the Puritan Book of Judges. No reasonable critic would expect to find much respecting religious affairs in such a work, covering three or four centuries in sixteen chapters, and devoting four of them to the exploits of Samson, the Israelitish Morrissey (we mean no disrespect to either champion: we make our apology to the shades of both). Whatever light the book will throw upon the subject we shall produce in due time.* We have said enough to show that Dr. Kuenen's argument, drawn from the *silence* of the book, is very weak, if not entirely destitute of force.

* See "Study of the Pentateuch," under "*Quotations from Judges*," page 141 of this volume.

The historical notices contained in I. Samuel, preceding the anointing of David, will require but a word of consideration. They were probably written by some earlier writer than the author of the Books of the Kings, and he may have continued the history to near the close of David's reign. The style is more diffuse than that of the author of Kings, and is freer from Aramæan or Chaldee words. What records he used, if any, he does not inform us; and the amount of credit which we give to his narrative will depend upon the probability of the events occurring under the circumstances described. Very strange things happen sometimes; and this rule, therefore, must be applied with great caution and modesty. Very little, if anything, respecting ecclesiastical affairs would be likely to be found in a brief description of the transition of the people from a state of anarchy and tribal rivalship and independence to the restraints of a monarchy and the authority of a central government. And what little there should be found would be such imperfect hints or such dissevered statements as would aid but little in forming a correct opinion of their religious rites and hierarchy. And if there were a ritual and a priesthood and an altar prescribed, it would be impossible in such stormy times to enforce or enjoy its observance, "every man for himself" doing what was right in his own eyes; and, as necessity knows no law, religious rites and ceremonies would be regarded or disregarded as circumstances compelled or permitted. If the appointed altar could not be reached, the sacrifice would be offered elsewhere; if the appointed priest could not be found, the next most worthy person would officiate; if the day appointed could not be observed, the next day most appropriate would be chosen. Laws would not be enforced, criminals would escape, crimes would be winked at. Whether any evidence whatever exists in these narratives of the existence of any ritual or code of forms of worship will be the subject of future examination.* It certainly would not disappoint a student of history to find little or nothing on the subject. He certainly would not decide categorically, as Dr. Kuenen has done, that there was no such ecclesiastical polity in existence, because at this particular period of anarchy it was in abeyance, or because in these scraps of civil history and accounts of insurrections it was not specially mentioned.

On the contrary, Dr. Kuenen maintains that the ritual contained in the Pentateuch could not have been in existence during this period, because no direct reference is made to it by these writers, and because so much was done which was in violation of it. But who does not know that laws are violated, customs disregarded, rites neglected? Who does not know that the Thirty-nine Articles of the Episcopal Church are Calvinistic, and that its preaching is largely Arminian? Was the ritual, so to speak, of the gospel less ignored by the Church 600 —1000 A.D. than the ritual of the Pentateuch from Joshua to Hezekiah, if you please, six centuries? The inference from comparative silence and disregard is not a safe nor a sound one, where that silence can be explained and that disregard accounted for, as can easily and satisfactorily be done during the period before us. The narratives relate almost exclusively to civil affairs,

---

*See "Study of the Pentateuch," under "*Quotations from Samuel*," page 136 of this volume.

and, for the most part, in the briefest manner; and the people were governed by passions and appetites made greedy and lawless by centuries of slavery and suffering in the midst of the grossest idolatry, and therefore spurned the restraints of law and the denial of idol-worship. A people cannot be lifted in an hour or a century from ignorance, brutality, and idolatry to knowledge, refinement, and spiritual worship; and well may it have taken a millennium of struggle and failure and worshipping of asheras and Baals before these degraded slaves could accept a "spiritual monotheism," and burn their asheras, and understand that even their own ritual was an offence to God unless the heart was pure and the hands clean which observed it. We will quote, as we can, such authority as De Wette in support of our position: "The observance or non-observance of particular laws, the appearance or non-appearance of particular legal institutions, in a certain period, can prove nothing, either for or against the existence of a written law book."* We submit that the silence of these books respecting the existence and observance of the Mosaic ritual, and the few accounts of religious observances not conforming to it, are no valid proof that it did not exist, especially as against the later tradition of the nation. We shall in due time show that perfect silence does not pervade these books. We are now only dealing with Dr. Kuenen's argument.

Respecting the Books of Ezra and Nehemiah to which allusion has just been made, a few words must be said; for in these very brief fragments of the condition of the Israelites for about a century, 537—434

* Parker's De Wette, § 162, *s*.

B.C., after their return from captivity, we may find some evidence of Dr. Kuenen's remarkable theory. He thinks he does. Let us examine the books, and see what it is worth, if indeed there is any.

It is evident that the best-conditioned and most religious of the captives, those to whom "Jerusalem was their chief joy," would undertake the long desert journey, and attempt to rebuild the city and temple, and re-establish the services of the fathers. They were among the most intelligent and devoted of their race, and would be most solicitous to establish in its purity the worship of the fathers, and to render perfect obedience to those laws whose violation had been visited by the destruction of their city and the captivity of its citizens. The first company which went up under the lead of Zerubbabel as civil governor or king, and of Jeshua as high-priest and head of religious affairs, were accompanied by all the servants serving in the old temple worship, and carried back the vessels which Nebuchadnezzar had taken from the temple and carried to Babylon. There were about fifty thousand souls, — men, women, and children. On arriving at Jerusalem, they immediately erected an altar, and at once commenced worship in accordance with the custom of the fathers, offering sacrifices "*as it is written in the law of Moses, the man of God.*" They either had with them a written ritual, or they knew there was one which they remembered, and which they observed. They also arranged their singers after "*the ordinance of David, King of Israel*," showing by this act also strict regard to the customs of the fathers. How Dr. Kuenen can say that they did not sing, but only "hoarsely shouted," cannot be reconciled with Ezra iii., 11, which says, "And they, the priests in their apparel with trumpets, and the Levites, the sons of Asaph, with their cymbals, sung together by course in praising and giving thanks unto the LORD; because he is good, for his mercy endureth forever toward Israel"; and so thrilled were the multitude, as they heard again the old temple anthems, that they "shouted with a great shout, and the noise was heard afar off." There is not a shadow of evidence but that all this ritual service was familiar to them, and that it was observed as it was "written in the law of Moses, and after the ordinance of David." Having finished their temple, after twenty years' hindrance and hard labor, it was dedicated by the sacrifice of "bullocks and lambs and he-goats; by the priests in their divisions, and the Levites in their courses, for the service of God, ... *as it is written in the book of Moses.*" They kept "the passover and the feast of unleavened bread." They also "kept the feast of tabernacles, *as it is written;* according *to the custom*, daily burnt offerings" were offered. There is not the slightest hint that the temple service was not continued for fifty-eight years, till Ezra and his company arrived, without intermission, and in accordance with the "custom" of the fathers, and as "it was *written in the book of Moses.*"

Did Ezra introduce any change? Did he make "known and impose upon the Jewish nation priestly ordinances, *now for the first time*" commanded? Were rites now introduced of which Zerubbabel and Jeshua, the king and high-priest, and these devoted exiles *knew nothing*, as Dr. Kuenen affirms?* Let us read

* Vol. II., p. 231.

what the fragments of history preserved in the Book of Ezra tell us on this subject. Ezra "was a ready scribe in the *law of Moses, which the Lord God of Israel had given*" (Ezra vii., 6); and he was a priest, great-grandson of Hilkiah, who found the "book of the law" in the reign of Josiah, if the genealogy is correct; and "Ezra had prepared his heart to *seek the law of the Lord and to do it*, and to teach in Israel statutes and judgments." After a few days, "the princes," who apparently had succeeded Zerubbabel in the government, complained to Ezra, who came with authority from the Persian King, that the people had intermarried, *contrary to the law*, with the neighboring people. Ezra at once set about a reform, and a covenant was made to put away their unlawful wives. "And let it be done," they said, "*according to the law.*" "Some of these wives had children," not all. The whole number of guilty persons was one hundred and thirteen only, out of a population of over fifty thousand. Not a great number, certainly, if we consider the condition of the people and the strength of the temptation. This act of Ezra is founded upon no new interpretation of "*the law written by Moses*," which had been the law of the nation from the beginning; much less was it a new law of Ezra's.

Nehemiah now visits Jerusalem. In his prayer for guidance before he left the palace in Shushan, he confesses that "we have not kept the commandments, nor the statutes, nor the judgments, which *thou commandest thy servant Moses*," as if he knew no code but the old code of the fathers,—the code which the returned people had used for three generations, "*as written in the book of the law of Moses.*" Complaint was made to Nehemiah that the poor were oppressed by the "usury" demanded, and some of them had lost their homes by the unlawful and cruel exaction of creditors. Nehemiah was "angry, and rebuked the nobles and the rulers, and directed them to leave off this usury and to restore their olive yards and houses." And they promised under oath to do so. After some years, Ezra again appears upon the stage as a teacher of the law. The people felt their need of fuller instruction. He used for this purpose "*the book of the law of Moses*, which the Lord had commanded for Israel." The same book evidently which Zerubbabel had used seventy years before, and of which Nehemiah spoke in his prayer. This old "book of the law" Ezra read and explained to the people. The devout wept when they learned how they had sinned. The direction to dwell in "booths" in the seventh month seems to have been new to them, though they had kept the "feast of the tabernacles" since their return.

A farther separation takes place from "strangers." In the ninth chapter, a synopsis of the history of the people is given as recorded in the Pentateuch, showing that the "law" which was read was supposed to have had its origin at that time; and the covenant of the fathers is renewed by the children, "to walk in God's law, *which was given by Moses, the servant of God*, and to observe and do all the commandments of the Lord, ... and not to give our daughters unto the people of the land, nor take their daughters for our sons." And they promise to contribute to the support of the Levites "*as it is written in the law.*" All this is in the Pentateuch, and is not spoken of as anything new. A selection of one man in ten is made by lot to dwell in Jerusalem. This is new; but it has nothing to do with the ritual. They further "*read in the book of Moses* that the Ammonite and the Moabite should not come into the congregation of God forever." They therefore "separated from Israel all the mixed multitude." Nehemiah, also, reformed the acts and labors of the people on the Sabbath, to conform to the "custom" of the fathers. This is all. There is not the slightest shade of evidence that Ezra introduced an entire new code of laws, never before known, but the contrary. A few new arrangements are made to meet the new condition, in which the people find themselves; but there is not a hint that anything new to which they were not accustomed, save in three or four instances at the most, and these unimportant, was added to "*the book of the law given by Moses.*" It is incredible that no breath of opposition should have been felt against this code, if it had not been what it claimed to be, "*the law given by Moses.*" It is incredible, if there had been any opposition on this ground, that no hint of it, nor the slightest trace of it, should be found in these accounts of the reorganization of the national worship. The very slight changes in a few forms, which changed circumstances compelled, by no means furnish proof or justify the suspicion that the whole post-captivity code was the invention of priests for selfish purposes, with Ezra at their head; and that he had the hardihood to proclaim to the people that it was the very "law given by Moses," and "written" by him, and observed by their fathers, and whose violation, at last, was the cause of their captivity and renewed obedience to which would now make them prosperous; and that the people were so stupid as not to detect the fraud and expose the deceivers, and visit them with swiftest and severest punishment; or, if they did, that all record of this detection, opposition, and punishment, should have been lost by accident, or erased by design, from both history and prophecy. That the *historical books* contain no evidence of such a ritual-forgery palmed off upon the returned exiles, we have already fully shown. Nay, more: we have shown that every fragment of these annals, every shred of the story, informs us that this "law" was the old law, and that this ritual was the ritual of the fathers. We turn now to examine the teachings of the prophets during this period, to see whether Dr. Kuenen's appeal to them in support of his theory is of any more value than his appeal to history. Unless we utterly mistake, this support will also prove to be a broken reed which will pierce him through who leans upon it.

(1) Dr. Kuenen says "that when Ezekiel, in the year 572 B.C., wrote his description of the new Israelitish State (chaps. xl.—xlviii.), no written regulations for religious worship, no complete priestly legislation, yet existed." And he says further, "that no evident trace of these laws, or of the spirit which they breathe, is to be found in the prophecies which saw the light toward the end of the captivity,—about 538 B.C.*

Ezekiel we will notice first, as being probably the earliest of the group, then the later Isaiah and Zechariah, and then Haggai and Malachi. Ezekiel was not

* Vol. II., p. 153.

of the company carried to Babylon. He was a dweller on the remote river Chebar. The description which he gives (chaps. xl.—xlviii.) of the division of the land among the returned exiles, whenever they should return, and of the temple they would build, is purely ideal, and as impracticable, should an attempt be made to make it real, as the throne or chariot of the Deity which he describes in chapter i. is impracticable. This Dr. Kuenen admits apparently, but he will not admit that Ezekiel would have given play to his imagination in describing the "ritual" of his ideal temple. Why not? Was the sacrifice more sacred than the altar? Was the priest's attire more holy than the "holy of holies"? Why, then, should the prophet restrain his pen in describing the "snuffers" and the "snuffer-trays" and the "tongs" and the robes, when he had not shrunk from describing ideally the altar and the holy place? The presumption is that he would not. "Why did he go into these minute descriptions of the ritual, if he had the Pentateuch? Why did he not content himself with a simple reference to the Mosaic laws?" asks Dr. Kuenen. If Ezekiel was here, we have no doubt he would reply, Because I was writing a poem, and wished to fill out my ideal state and temple and ritual in every particular. Besides, Ezekiel clings close to the forms and substance contained in the Pentateuch which he idealizes in his poem. Dr. Kuenen says "he was not acquainted with the whole of the Mosaic law. Deuteronomy and the still older book of the covenant are presupposed by him throughout, but nothing beyond these collections." Now the fact is this: by a careful collation of the passages and references which are found in Ezekiel, nearly the whole ritual as it is contained in the Pentateuch could be obtained. Ezekiel uses the whole of the ritual as it stands in the Pentateuch; that is, all which his work demanded. Could space be given, we would prove it by an examination of the passages quoted. It must suffice, however, to say that Ezekiel shows himself to be perfectly familiar with the "law of Moses" as recorded in the Pentateuch, writing in a distant part of the country, one hundred and fourteen years before Ezra went up to Jerusalem, and thirty-six years before the great migration under Zerubbabel, who had regard in offering sacrifices to what "was written in the law of Moses, the man of God," and who arranged the courses of the priests "as it is written in the book of Moses."*

(2) We turn to examine the support furnished to Dr. Kuenen's theory by the later, or "Deutero," Isaiah. This writer "lays special stress upon *Jahveh's oneness*"; he expresses most significantly his contempt of false gods; he is a strong "monotheist." There is not a passage which implies the non-existence of the ritual law or of the Pentateuch, but much to the contrary. He speaks of the worthlessness of the ritual unless the heart is in its observance; but this is evidence for the existence of the ritual, and not proof that it did not exist. As we shall have occasion to recur to this writer again before we finish this discussion, we waive farther examination of his work till then, having said sufficient to show that Dr. Kuenen's inference is unfounded.†

* For further proof, see "Study of the Pentateuch," under "*Ezekiel*," p. 105.
† See "Study of the Pentateuch," under "*Isaiah*," p. 112.

(3) But a word is necessary upon the writings of the later Zechariah. He was a contemporary of Zerubbabel, and the numerous visions which he describes assume the existence of the ritual, though no direct reference is made to it. Indeed, Dr. Kuenen does not appear to place much reliance upon his silence as valid evidence that the ritual was not in existence, and regarded as far as the circumstances would allow.

(4) The prophet Haggai, in the brief fragment of only two chapters of his writings which have come down to us, uses the language of the Pentateuch, and speaks of "the law," as respecting things "clean and unclean." Dr. Kuenen infers from chap. ii., 11, because the prophet directs the people to inquire "concerning the law" of the priests, that there were no "enactments of the written law": "only a priestly tradition existed." As if, because one was referred to the lawyer when he inquired after the "law" on a certain subject, we should infer that there was no statute, written law, but only the tradition of the bar. It so happens that the very point inquired about is stated and decided in Numbers xix., 11. Haggai furnishes no support to Dr. Kuenen's theory.

(5) The brief prophecy of Malachi, who was a contemporary of Nehemiah, is thought by Dr. Kuenen to give support to his theory, because he shows that "Ezra and Nehemiah in their attempt at reform met with strong opposition." The people violated the law in various ways, and some of them despised Jahveh's name. But this "law" which Malachi denounces the people for disregarding and violating is no forgery of the priesthood and Ezra, no new ritual palmed off

upon the nation by a conspiring hierarchy, Nehemiah assenting and abetting,— it was none other than "*the law of Moses,*" the servant of Jehovah, which God "*commanded him in Horeb for all Israel.*" If Malachi reproved the people, it was for transgressing the "*law as it was written by Moses*"; and, if the people opposed Ezra and Nehemiah, it was because they enforced against evil-doers "*the law as written by Moses,*" and not a fraudulent code of Ezra's. There is not a shadow of evidence that any opposition arose against the administration of these men because they introduced "new laws never before heard of"; but all the evidence that exists of the opposition itself as well as of its cause implies or affirms that it originated in the enforcement of laws whose violation was the cause of their captivity, and whose origin was in the ancient days, "*in Horeb,*" and whose author "*was Moses, the man of God.*"

The prophetical writings of this period not only give no countenance to Dr. Kuenen's theory, but they oppose it in letter as well as in spirit.

We have now examined the main reasons adduced by Dr. Kuenen in support of his hypotheses of the origin of the Pentateuch, as they are less frequently stated than implied in these volumes. To discuss every point affirmed or suggested, to challenge every statement which is doubtful or incorrect, to expose every fallacious inference from conceded facts, would demand as many volumes as the original work. We have omitted nothing vital to his argument.*

See Appendix B, page 66.

Thus far in the discussion, we have been laboring at a disadvantage. We have been proving a negative. We have been showing that the arguments adduced by Dr. Kuenen are not valid to sustain his theory of the late and forged composition of the Pentateuch. The positive argument for its antiquity and substantial genuineness does not appear. Dr. Kuenen's argument in support of his theory may be confuted, and yet his theory may be correct. We propose, therefore, to discuss the question positively and affirmatively, confuting his theory indirectly by an examination into the age and authorship of the so-called Books of Moses directly and critically, as we have confuted his arguments in support of it by testing their logical and historical value. We gird ourselves to the work in the assurance that the antiquity of the Pentateuch can be vindicated, and that the Mosaic origin of most of its contents can be established.

APPENDIX A.*

In *The Bible for Learners*, by Dr. H. Oort, Professor of Oriental Languages, etc., Amsterdam, and Dr. T. Hooykaas, pastor at Rotterdam, with the assistance of Dr. A. Kuenen, Professor of Theology at Leiden, there are abundant specimens of these "flimsiest speculations." I quote a few to justify to the reader the use of such language respecting the works of this school of critics.

"The tabernacle," Dr. Oort says, "never really existed, except in the imagination of the writer," who lived after the captivity. This writer must have been infatuated with this creation of his imagination, of "rams' skins dyed red," and "badger skins," and "fine-twined linen," and "loops and couplings, blue upon the edge, and taches and curtains of goats' hair, and boards of shittim wood, and two tenons on one board, and forty sockets of silver, two sockets under one board, and bars of shittim wood, five bars for the boards of the tabernacle on the one side, and five bars for the boards of the tabernacle on the other side, and the middle bar in the midst of the boards shall reach from end to end," etc.,— must have been infatuated, indeed, for he repeats the wearisome, dry details in the following chapters, which one has hardly patience to read once.

The "representation of the camp of the Israelites," as given in the Book of Numbers, we are told "the writer

* See page 8.

had invented and worked out himself." No truth is in it. We must class it with the historical "lies," for there is no doubt about the writer's intending that his readers should believe it was a true description of the work of Moses.

Dr. Oort tells "learners" that "the prophet Malachi [420–450 B.C.] is the first to use the expression 'law of Moses.'" Now, the title is used I. Kings ii., 3, and II. Kings xxiii., 25, books acknowledged by such critics as De Wette and Davidson to have been written about 550 B.C. And the title is also used by the writer of the Book of Joshua, placed by the same critics about 650 B.C., or two centuries earlier than Dr. Oort admits that the title was used. Dr. Oort tells "learners" that "the very name given to . . . the Mount of Sinai signifies the moon-god." We do not say that some modern critics are moon-struck, but the moon has as much influence on their criticism as it has on the meteorology of the rustic. Gesenius (Hebrew *Thesaurus, ad verb.*) says Sinai signifies "*lutum*," "mire"! Again, Dr. Oort tells "learners" that "the very name of the hero himself [Samson] signifies 'sun-god.'" Gesenius says it signifies "sunlike." These assertions need no comment. They admonish "learners" to choose judicious teachers, and to beware of disregarding truth, as the Hebrew writers are said to have done.

Dr. Oort seems disposed, at times, to give the worst interpretation possible to popular phraseology. For example, he says the proverb, as used in Ecclesiastes, "A living dog is better than a dead lion," means, "Life, though branded with infamy, is preferable to the most honorable of deaths"! The real meaning of the proverb is, while there is life there is capacity, activity, hope of change from misfortune and sorrow; but when dead we are good for nothing, can do nothing, can hope for nothing. " Infamy " is not said to be "preferable to death." So base a sentiment could not be found among the Ojibways.

We will take one of Dr. Oort's myths, and learn his style of interpretation. Solar myths are fashionable now among the critics; and the story of Samson opens a rich field for fancy to riot in, as Dr. Oort in his chapter on this Hebrew athlete illustrates. He opens his criticism with a reference to Osiris and Horos and Typhon and Herakles and Balder and Loki, original solar myths; and, as the "very name" of the hero "Samson" signifies "sun-god," the reader is admonished in the outset of the solar myth to be narrated. A rhetorical description, in his own language, is given of the interview of the angel and Manoah, the father of Samson. He then interprets : "Samson had long hair. These long hairs are rays of the sun. The angel who rises up in the flame of Manoah's sacrifice signifies the glow of the dawn that blazes against the heavens, and heralds the approach of the sun who brings to the world fresh life." This is rich, but there is richer in store. Dr. Oort gives a glowing description of Samson's exploits, "killing the lion," "getting honey from the carcass," and his riddle about it. A very simple thing for a fellow like Samson to do. Now for the mythical interpretation. The "lion" is a "sign in the zodiac." "Samson rends the lion; that is to say, the sun passes through the constellation of that name." ... "How did sweet food, honey, proceed from the strong and ravenous lion?" ... "When the sun passes through the lion, the bees make their combs; and, when he leaves it, the honey is ready." Is not this richer? Instead of saying, what was not at all improbable, that a swarm of bees had made honey in the hollow, bone-covered portion of the fleshless remains of the slain beast, we are directed to the constellations for an answer to the riddle. It is no wonder that the Philistines did not guess the riddle, and it is a wonder that Samson was such a fool as to think they did when they did not; for they only thought of the real beast: they had no zodiacal signs in mind.

Now for the story of the jackals (foxes), tied "tail to tail, with a burning torch between them," and sent among the Philistines' wheat all ready to harvest, which so provoked them that they followed him to Lehi, where he was delivered up by his friends, who feared the vengeance of the Philistines, bound with two new ropes. But, when the Philistines shouted and came upon him, he snapped the ropes, and seized the jaw-bone of an ass, and slew them by the thousand; and they fled; and, when he was thirsty, he cried to Yahweh, and "God split the hollow of the jaw-bone, and water flowed out from it to drink." One word of criticism before proceeding to give the mythical interpretation of this exploit. The water did not flow from the hollow in the jaw-bone of the ass, used by Samson in beating off the Philistines, but from a hollow, a spring, in Lehi, the place where the squabble was. Now, the Hebrew word Lehi signifies "jaw"; and Dr. Oort thinks the Lehi where the spring of water was was the jaw-bone of the ass, and not the place Lehi. Our translators made a mistake in translating the name;

"But God clave a hollow place that was in the jaw," when they should have said, "a hollow place that was in Lehi." There was a spring of water in that place, Lehi, which Samson found and drank from. This is all.

But it is time to give Dr. Oort's mythical interpretation. In "the reddish-brown jackals, with torches between their tails, we easily recognize the lurid thunder-clouds, from the projecting points [tails?] of which lightning flashes seem to dart." "When he has triumphed over his foes, the sun-god no longer uses the thunder-cloud as a weapon, but makes the rain pour out of it. This explains why Samson threw away his weapon after the victory, and that a spring rose from the hollow of the jaw-bone." This is certainly richer still!

Patience! But one more specimen remains. Samson loses his locks by the betrayal of Delilah, and grinds in the mill of the Philistines, among the women. His hair grows again; he is taken out to make sport for the curious multitude, who so pile the roof of the building that, by a push upon a couple of its pillars, it fell, and killed many besides Samson. All very probable and intelligible, and substantially true, past all reasonable question. Now for the solar-myth interpretation. Losing his locks in the winter months, "the sun-god is gradually encompassed by his enemies, mist and darkness. He loses all his power and glory. Gradually his strength returns, and at last he reappears, ... and, in the end, triumphs over his enemies once more. This final victory is represented by the scene in the Temple of Dagon." The sun dies every year, and comes to life again; but "Samson was buried between Zorah and

Eshtahol, in the burying-place of Manoah, his father," and we hear no more of him. Such is the interpretation of the stories of the Bible commended to "learners." It is true that this is the most extravagant one of all that have come under my observation; but the only reason why others are not as extravagant seems to be that no others furnish such opportunity for the revels of imagination. If this is criticism, what would be travesty?

An instance of the way the author has of charging the Hebrew writers with disregard of truth, and of falsifying their own records, is found in his account of the story of Korah.* "A later priest," he says, "who accepted the story as historical, was sadly perplexed by the fact that Korah's family not only still existed, but was held in high honor. He therefore took the liberty of making a note to the effect that Korah's children did not perish with him (Numbers xxvi., 11), thereby contradicting the story itself, which expressly says that both he and his were destroyed" (Numbers xvi., 32). Now, the original account does *not* say that the *children* of Korah were swallowed up. It does not even say that *Korah* was swallowed up. It says that "Dathan and Abiram came out and stood in the door of their tents, and their wives and their sons and their little children; ... and the earth opened her mouth and swallowed *them* up, and *their* houses, and all the *men* that appertained to Korah, and all *their* goods. *They*, and all that appertained to *them*, went down alive into the pit." ... Not a word is said that Korah was there with Dathan and Abiram when the earth opened. It is *nowhere* said

* Vol. II., page 523.

that Korah or his children were swallowed up. It is nowhere said that Korah, himself, was killed, either by the opening of the earth or by the "fire that came out from the Lord and consumed the two hundred and fifty men that offered incense" "at the door of the tabernacle of the congregation." But, as Moses had told Korah the day before to be present with his company at that place, it is a fair inference that he was one of the two hundred and fifty who were "consumed by fire from the Lord at the door of the tabernacle," while Dathan and Abiram and their families were swallowed up in another part of the camp, where were the tents of Reubenites. So far is it, therefore, from being true that Hebrew writers "concerned themselves very little with the question whether what they narrated really happened so or not," that they excelled, in accuracy of writing and scrupulous regard to facts, some of their modern readers and commentators.

APPENDIX B.*

Some of Dr. Kuenen's affirmations are too important to be passed by in entire silence.

(I.) Dr. Kuenen affirms (Vol. II., p. 299) "that the Deuteronomist considers *all* Levites, without distinction, qualified to fill the priestly office," and "that a reconciliation of Deuteronomy with Exodus — Numbers is not to be thought of." This, he affirms, is certain "from Deuteronomy x., 8, 9; and xviii., 1–8, where he [the Deuteronomist] expresses himself quite unambiguously." . . . "He directly contradicts them [Exodus—Numbers] . . . and expressly allows (Deuteronomy xviii., 6, 7) that which, according to the priestly lawgiver (Numbers xviii., 3), is punished with death."

We take distinct issue with Dr. Kuenen on this point. In Deuteronomy xviii., 6, 7, we read, "If a Levite come from any of thy gates out of all Israel where he sojourned, and come with all the desire of his mind unto the place which the Lord shall choose, there he shall minister in the name of the Lord his God, *as all his brethren the Levites do*, which stand before the Lord." Now what says Numbers xviii., 2, 3? "And thy [Aaron's] brethren of the tribe of thy father, bring them with thee, that . . . they may minister unto thee; but *thou* and *thy* sons with thee shall minister *before the tabernacle of witness*, and *they* shall keep thy charge and the *charge of all the tabernacle;* only they shall *not* come

* See page 57.

nigh the *vessels of the sanctuary and the altar*, that neither they, nor ye also, die." And further on in this chapter many specific duties of the Levites, as distinguished from those of the priests, are enumerated. Where, we ask with emphasis, does Numbers "expressly contradict" Deuteronomy? What does Deuteronomy "expressly allow" which Numbers "punishes with death"? Both direct that Levites may serve at the tabernacle, Numbers specifying their duties, Deuteronomy only saying that the persons specified *"should serve as all the Levites do"*; that is, as directed in Numbers. We renew our question with stronger emphasis, Where is the " direct contradiction"?

Now let us examine the *first* affirmation that *"all* Levites, without distinction, [were] qualified to fill the priestly office," according to Deuteronomy viii., 9; xviii., 1–8. We have already quoted the important portion of the latter passage, and have only to remark that all attempts to build up a theory of the Jewish priesthood and the identity of the office of the priest and the Levite, because of the use of the phrase, "'The priests, the Levites," are futile. All priests were Levites, but *"all"* Levites were not qualified for priests; and this idiomatic phrase proves only that priests were Levites. A critical examination of this Hebrew idiom would take too much space, and lead us into details too dry and minute to interest our readers; and we refer them to the *constructio asyndeta* of the Hebrew grammars. We turn, therefore, to notice the other passage, which proves that *"all* Levites, without distinction, [were] qualified to fill the priestly office," Deuteronomy x., 8, 9. It reads thus: "At that time [at Mount Sinai] the Lord separated the tribe of Levi to bear the ark of the covenant of the Lord, to stand before the Lord to minister to him, and to bless in his name unto this day. Wherefore Levi hath no part nor inheritance with his brethren; the Lord is his inheritance, according as the Lord thy God promised him." What is there in this passage to show that "all" Levites were or might be priests? Not a line. The duty of the *tribe* of Levi is specified in the briefest manner, including the service of *both* priests and Levites, into which two classes the tribe is elsewhere said to be divided. "The reconciliation of Deuteronomy with Exodus — Numbers is not to be thought of," therefore, only because there is nothing to reconcile. Where there is no contradiction, there is no demand for conciliation. Dr. Kuenen's inference, therefore, that, since the Deuteronomist makes no distinction between the priest and Levite, he must have written before the "priestly ritual" of Exodus — Numbers and of Ezra was composed, is without support. Dr. Kuenen has mistaken an eddy for the current.*

(II.) Dr. Kuenen says again (Vol. II., p. 116), "Ezekiel is the first to desire other rules [than that all Levites might officiate as priests] *for the future:* after the return of Israel to her native land, 'the sons of Zadok' shall be the only lawful priests." But it is evident from the context (Ezekiel xliv., 10 – xlv.) that

* The statement, *Unitarian Review*, Nov. 1880, p. 937, that, "before this captivity, the terms 'priest' and 'Levite' are synonymous," is incorrect, as shown "(III.)"; and another writer echoes Kuenen's statement to the same effect, and further informs us that Kuenen "revised his whole scheme of Israel's history" on account of this supposed synonymousness of "priest" and "Levite." A pyramid on its apex, surely. See "The Levitical Priests," by Curtis.

Ezekiel had reference in this passage to the Levites, and priests of the family of Aaron, who had served at the altars of false gods in the reigns of Hezekiah and Josiah, and who had thus forfeited their claim to their official position; and as the "sons of Zadok" only of the family of Aaron remained loyal to Jehovah, they alone could officiate as priests. The most sacred services of the temple could be performed by them alone. Ezekiel desires no new rule. He only enforces an old one that those who forsake Jehovah and serve at the altars of false gods shall not serve at his altar. Dr. Kuenen is betrayed into this error by his not seeing that the priests are sometimes spoken of as Levites of whom they formed a part when the writer refers to the position and duties of the *tribe* as a body. And while in some instances it must be confessed that the sacred writers are not so clear as is desirable, yet nothing but an "assumed" theory could have led the author so far astray.

(III.) Again, Dr. Kuenen says (Vol. I., p. 325), "In David's days, no one thought of either the descendants of Aaron or the Levites being the only persons competent to discharge the functions of priests." This is a remarkable statement to make, when not the name of a person acting as priest is mentioned who is not a descendant of Aaron. The legitimate inference is that, where names are not mentioned, the "priests" who are officiating at the altar are the posterity of Aaron. Priests and their services are mentioned frequently during the reign of David by the writer of the Books of Samuel and Kings, and not a hint is given that they are not Aaronic.

(IV.) Dr. Kuenen says (Vol. I., p. 208): "*In the*

eighth century B.C., the prophet of Jahveh has become a writer. . . . It does not appear that the older prophets . . . thought of writing down what they had spoken." Yet we read that the "acts of David and Solomon," in the ninth and tenth centuries B.C., were "written by Nathan, the prophet," and also "in the visions of Iddo, the seer," and also in "the book of the prophet Gad, David's seer" (I. Chronicles xxix., 29; II. Chronicles ix., 29). The only marvel is that so much, not that so little, of the early miscellaneous literature of the Hebrews was preserved, when we remember the fortune of that people.

(V.) Dr. Kuenen says (Vol. I., p. 273), "Probably not one of the Psalms is from David's hand." So destructive a critic as Hitzig claims that he wrote ten certainly, perhaps more. And Ewald claims fifteen, and probably several others. Davidson claims still more. So does Eichorn, and Dr. Noyes, also. A dozen eminent Hebrew scholars might be named who believe that David wrote from twenty to eighty of the Psalms; but it is not necessary. Every student of the Hebrew Scriptures knows them. But general readers are widely and sadly misled by such statements, and judicious, reliable scholars do not make them.

(VI.) Dr. Kuenen is very confident that he can pick out the portions of the "Book of Origins," or the Elohim document, from Exodus — Numbers; and he confides in the accuracy of his dissection with an assurance which is surprising to one who has made the subject a study. The fact is, *no* confidence can be placed in any of these attempts to find and define the supposed documents of which some writers affirm that these books are composed. We have given the subject a careful and most minute study, and we say without hesitation that all these attempts are abortive. Some specimens will be given taken from Kuenen (Vol. II., p. 163 —). "Exodus xii., 1–23, 28, 37 (?), 40–51, are from his [Elohist's] hand." Now, this writer calls the Supreme Being, in Hebrew, Elohim, God, as distinguished from the later writer who calls the Supreme Being, in Hebrew, Jehovah, Lord. This is a "chief characteristic" of his style. In this passage, quoted by Dr. Kuenen as written by the Elohist, the name "Jehovah" is used *fifteen* times and "Elohim" not *once*. In another passage, "Exodus xxv., 1; xxxi., 17," Jehovah is used *forty* times and Elohim but *three* times. Theodore Parker says, "I would rather consider the whole passage as Jehovistic." Again, "Exodus xxxv.–xl.," Jehovah is used *thirty-three* times and Elohim *once*. Theodore Parker says, "To me, this passage seems Jehovistic throughout." Again, "Leviticus viii.–x.," Jehovah is used *forty* times, Elohim *not once*. Again, "Numbers xv.–xix.," Jehovah is used *fifty-seven* times and Elohim *twice*. Once more, "Numbers xxvi.–xxxi.," Jehovah is used *fifty-two* times and Elohim but *once*. It is not necessary to extend this note further. The "chief characteristic" of the Elohim document almost entirely disappears in the passages attributed to the Elohist writer by Dr. Kuenen, and the "chief characteristic" of the Jehovistic writer is found in them. This is sufficient to show the fallacy of the whole criticism; for, if the "chief characteristic" of one of the theoretical documents is found to be almost universally used in the other in practice, either the theory or the practice is sadly at fault.

A STUDY OF THE PENTATEUCH.

A STUDY OF THE PENTATEUCH.

INTRODUCTION.

The Pentateuch, as well as other writings claiming a high antiquity, has been made to pass the fiery ordeal of criticism since the revival of Oriental learning, and, like not a few of them, has been denied the venerable age which had before been awarded to it. I do not complain that these writings have been tried in so purifying a fire. Nor will I complain that there has been some rashness manifested in this process of purification, since, in all first attempts, more or less imperfection must exist. But I have no doubt that it will be found in the end, after thorough scholarship and laborious research have done their work, that many of those writings, whose antiquity has been denied, will again be installed in their original places of reverence and age. The tendency is in that direction, even at this time; and it will grow stronger and stronger as the discoveries of scholars in the ruins of the ancient cities give decisive evidence of the general, and sometimes minute, accuracy of the accounts which these books contain, and of a literature as abundant, as various, and as copious as is found in the Pentateuch.

There was a time, and it is not long since, when the history of Herodotus was looked upon as largely mythical, as composed of "tales imposed upon the credulity of the Father of History"; but almost every modern discovery goes to confirm the general accuracy of Herodotus, and convict the incredulity of his critics. The same is true of other ancient documents, and fragments of documents, which have come down to our day. Thorough modern research seems to be fast confirming the old opinion respecting the antiquity and authenticity of the writings which claim to be the work of ancient men.

The Old Testament writings have shared to some extent the fate of the writings of Herodotus and other ancient authors. Their historical parts have been put to the test of criticism, and have been declared wanting. But recent discoveries and more thorough examination are confirming their general accuracy, and winning back to them a continually increasing portion of the confidence which they formerly commanded. Especially is this true of the Pentateuch. The writings of Moses, as they are usually called, have been subjected to the closest scrutiny by the most profound scholars. Perhaps no work claiming its origin in remote antiquity has passed through such an ordeal, and with such various results. In the first instance, a very modern date was given to it. The age of Ezra was reported by some as that in which it first saw the light. The date of its origin has, however, been receding; and generally an antiquity considerably higher is now conceded to it by most of the same school of critics.

But it is not my purpose to write a history of the progress of criticism upon the age and authenticity of the Pentateuch. I have made these remarks to notify my readers of the present tendency of that kind of criticism, which has been, by some defenders of the ancient records, styled "destructive," that they may be better able to appreciate the force of the arguments which I propose to adduce in this study, to show that the Pentateuch is of the age of Moses; that there are reasons, by no means without weight, for the opinion that the first five books of the Old Testament, called the Pentateuch, were in the main compiled and written either by Moses himself or by one or more of his contemporaries, perhaps under his direction, or, at the latest, by his immediate successors. It is no part of my plan to prove the authenticity of these books,— the truth of the statements made in them,— though incidentally I shall touch that subject. My object is a single and simple one. I wish to present the reasons which have induced many of the most eminent scholars and the great mass of believers, so far as they have had reasons to give for their belief, for attributing the Pentateuch to an author or authors of the Mosaic Age. Nor do I propose to show or maintain that these writings have come down to us without damage, in their original state precisely. I shall assume that they have met with the same fate in their transmission to our age which has befallen all other ancient writings. Nor shall I claim for them any inspiration, in any sense of that word. I shall examine them as I would any other writings of antiquity.

I propose this only as my theme,— to examine the evidence of the origin and age of the first five books in our Bible, commonly called the Pentateuch. I call this essay a Study, because it is the result of my own personal investigation extending over a period approaching half a century, and during a portion of which time my duty as teacher at Meadville required me to read the Pentateuch, as well as the rest of the Hebrew literature contained in the Old Testament, annually with the students; and nothing has surprised or pained me more of late years than the careless facility with which even men having the reputation of scholarship copy and adopt the statements of others, especially if they have come over the sea, without verifying them; and are not only led far astray themselves, which would be little, but they lead far astray multitudes of others who confide in them, just as if they were authority, and knew themselves, by their own studies, whereof they affirm. The credulous, confiding public is flooded with books and pamphlets written without knowledge and published without thought. It is a very easy thing to do to rewrite a dry, dull book into a fresh and attractive one, and to scatter broadcast in volume or pamphlet, in essay or sermon, the crude, wild, baseless theories and hypotheses of persons who, like the old Athenians, have nothing to do but to tell some new thing, or startle men with some astonishing discovery, or mortify them with some bold irreverence. No responsibility seems to be felt for the influence of opinions, and little regard is paid oftentimes to truth. There is hot haste to get every new hypothesis, the last guess, before the public. It goes up like a rocket, fizzing and sparkling, to the admiration of the on-lookers, but soon grows dim, fades away, disappears, and disappoints.

No such charge as haste or want of care can be

attributed to the preparation and publication of this Study. Want of skill, want of knowledge, may be its vital, fatal defects. Had I known more, I should have escaped my errors; had I delayed publication longer, I might have been wiser, and not have printed my conclusions. But such as I have, after these long years of inquiry, I give, in the hope that my contribution to this branch of Biblical criticism will not be wholly in vain.

Before entering upon the examination of the subject in hand, however, it will be necessary to give an outline of the construction and contents of the work which we are to examine, that the course of our inquiry may be clearly understood. The Pentateuch is composed of a sketch of the lives of the three great ancestors of the Hebrew people,— Abraham, Isaac, and Jacob, Genesis xii.-l.,— preceded by a sketch of the creation and the flood, and genealogies of the descendants of Adam in the line of Abraham to him (Genesis i.-xi.); and followed, after an interval of centuries, with an account of the residence of the Hebrews in Egypt and their escape from bondage to Mount Sinai (Exodus i.-xix.). All this is historical, and, excepting what is in Exodus, relates to what transpired before the birth of Moses, and may have been the work of some other person, even after his death. Nor is it probable that what is contained in Exodus up to the twentieth chapter was written by him. Nor by any one else was it written at the time the events recorded took place, and *may* not have been written for a century or more afterward. Moses and all the other leaders were too busily engaged in rescuing the people from the Egyptians, and providing for their wants and organizing them into some orderly body, to undertake any literary labors. The laws given and the ritual prescribed and the place of worship erected, and its furniture, and the priest's duties and garments, are described and recorded. (Exodus xx.— Numbers x., 10). This portion was written as the laws were given and as the events transpired, day by day, at Sinai. Whatever is written respecting their wanderings, till they arrived on the eastern bank of the Jordan (Numbers x., 11–xxxvi.), was written as the events took place, either by Moses or by his scribe, or by both. The closing addresses by Moses, and the amendments and additions to the laws contained in them, were written by Moses himself or under his direction, by his scribes (Deuteronomy i.-xxxi.). There is no conclusive internal evidence that he did not compose the song contained in the thirty-second chapter, and the blessings in the thirty-third; but some other hand of course gave the account of his death and burial in the thirty-fourth chapter. The whole Pentateuch, however, was written before any other books that have come down to us, as the style, the "archaic language," shows, and will be illustrated hereafter.

This inquiry respecting the origin and age of the Pentateuch may be pursued, if one pleases, as a purely literary one; for the Mosaic dispensation is not ours, nor is the Law our rule of life. Whatever may prove true in regard to the Pentateuch, our relations to God, to Christ, and to man, are unchanged. Whether the Law was of human or of divine origin, we are, as Christians, to obey Christ, and accept the "substance," of which the Law, at the best, was only a "shadow." As a purely literary inquiry, therefore, I shall discuss them.

Three distinct questions present themselves for consideration in opening our inquiry: Is the Pentateuch as old as the time of Moses? Is Moses its author? Does it contain a reliable account of the revelation which God made to the Jews? The first of these questions may be answered in the affirmative, and yet both the others be answered in the negative. The first two may be answered in the affirmative, and the last in the negative. The second may be answered in the negative, and the first and last in the affirmative. We can suppose Moses wrote the book and wrote incorrectly. We can suppose it to be of the Mosaic Age, and yet not written by him. We can suppose that, though not written by him, it contains the truth.

In this Study, I propose to examine and answer only the first question: Is the Pentateuch as *old* as the time of Moses? The inquiry will be divided into two parts: (1) *the historical indications of the existence of the book;* and (2) *the evidence to be derived from its internal character,*— or the external and internal evidence. I shall commence with the former.

PART I.

EXTERNAL EVIDENCE.

In tracing the historical references to this work, we must have regard to the character of the writings in which the references are contained, and to the state of mind which the people were in to whom these writings were addressed. Where a people are well acquainted with a book, the references to it will be incidental rather than direct, implied rather than expressed. The Pentateuch, in the time of our Saviour, was so well known that it was not necessary to be definite in describing the book when references were made to it. The copy used, the page from which the quotation was taken, or to which reference was made, were not stated. The writer or speaker thought he had been sufficiently explicit if he had said "The Law" or "The Law of Moses" or "The Book of the Law." More frequently in that age, the Pentateuch was called only "The Law." Let us, then, trace back from this period, in which the Pentateuch was undeniably called "The Law" when reference was made to it, indications of its existence in still earlier periods. And if we find references made to "The Law" and to "The Book of the Law" and to "The Law of Moses" and to "The Law of the Lord," we are bound to infer, unless overpowering reasons to the contrary can be given, that the Pentateuch is the book referred to; and especially are we bound to infer this, if *quotations* are made from the book referred to which are contained in the Pentateuch as we now have it, or as it existed at the time the quotations were made. These statements, if reduced to a canon of criticism, would give the following law of historical inquiry, which I believe to be correct; namely, *if we find that an ancient book is referred to, in all later works, by the name which is now given to it, and that references are made to it, and that quotations are made from its contents, such substantially as we now find in it, then the proper, the necessary conclusion is that the book is the same as that which we possess.*

This law of historical criticism I intend to apply to this inquiry respecting the antiquity of the Pentateuch in substantially the same form as that in which it existed in the time of Christ. I propose to go back, step by step, examining all the writings relating to the subject which have come down to our time, that we may learn whether they refer to the "Book of Moses," and, if so, in what manner. If we find such a book alluded to, named, quoted from, in the writings which have come down to us from the Jewish people, then the conclusion is that the book is at least as old as any of these writings, just as a traveller who has ascended the Nile from Alexandria to its outflow from a lake in central Africa would be sure he had found its source.

SECTION I. FROM CHRIST TO MALACHI.

I begin with the first Book of Esdras, which was probably written a short time before the birth of Christ. It speaks of the "Book of Moses," of "The Law of Moses," of "The Law of the Lord," and of "The

Law." That in the last instance a *book* is meant is clear from the rest of the passage: after Esdras had brought "The Law of Moses," "When he had *opened the Law*, they stood up" (ix., 46).

The first Book of Maccabees was written about one hundred years before Christ. "The Book of the Law" is spoken of (iii., 48), and "The Law" is very frequently alluded to in it. The Book of Ecclesiasticus was written about a century before the Book of Maccabees, according to the more probable opinion. In this, we find reference to "The Law which Moses commanded" (xxiv., 23), to "The Book of the Covenant of the Most High God," to "The Law of God," and to "The Law" very frequently. The translator of this book, who lived about seventy years later, speaks of "The Law," referring to the Pentateuch, five times in his short preface. One hundred years earlier than this book was written, the Septuagint translation was made; and, one hundred years before the Septuagint translation was made, the Samaritan Pentateuch was in existence. How much earlier than this it existed, I do not now attempt to decide. But that it existed as early as four hundred years before Christ there is no good reason to doubt. I have now gone back to the time of the Prophet Malachi. From his time down to the time of the son of Sirach, who composed the Book of Ecclesiasticus, we have probably no Jewish writings.

What they were accustomed to call the Pentateuch, when they referred to it by name, we cannot tell. It was in existence during this period we know; for the Septuagint translation was made, and the Samaritan Pentateuch was in existence. Back to the time of Malachi, it is very easy to trace the use of the Pentateuch as it existed in the time of Christ. There can be no mistake respecting it.

SECTION II. FROM MALACHI TO EZRA.

Let us now examine the books which are extant which were written *after* the return from the captivity, or rather those which *give an account* of the nation after its return from the captivity to the time of Malachi; for I will omit a consideration of the testimony of the Books of Chronicles for the present. The prophecies of Malachi, Zechariah, and Haggai, and the histories contained in Ezra and Nehemiah, cover a period of about one hundred and fifty years, extending back to five hundred and thirty-two years before Christ. Malachi exhorts the people to "remember the Law of Moses." He accuses the priests of being "partial in the Law," and of causing many to stumble at "The Law," and tells them that the people should seek "The Law" at the mouth of the priest (iv., 4; ii., 7, 8, 9). Haggai is directed by the Lord to ask the "priest concerning the Law" (ii., 11). Zechariah accuses the people of making "their hearts as an adamant stone, lest they should hear the Law" (vii., 12). The particular sins of which these prophets reproach the people are violations of precepts contained in the Pentateuch, and the virtues which they approve are founded on obedience to the laws found in it.

But we find much more distinct reference to the Pentateuch in the Books of Nehemiah and Ezra than in these poetical books. In the eighth chapter of the Book of Nehemiah there is a very full account of "The Book of the Law of Moses." A summary may be given in a few words, in which the various names by which this book was called may be included. The people spake to "Ezra the scribe to bring the Book of the Law of Moses, . . . and he brought the Law . . . and read therein, . . . and the ears of all the people were attentive unto the Book of the Law. . . . And Ezra opened the Book," and he appointed many others who "caused the people to understand the Law. . . . So they read in the Book of the Law of God distinctly. . . . And the people wept when they heard the words of the Law. . . . Also he read in the Book of the Law of God." In the tenth chapter, we read of "God's law given by the hand of Moses," and of that which "is written in the Law." In the thirteenth chapter, it is said, "They read in the Book of Moses." These passages show us most clearly that this book was called by different names, and that one of them was simply "The Law." The passages quoted in Nehemiah from "The Book of the Law" are found in the Pentateuch. Indeed, the Samaritan Pentateuch was nearly contemporaneous with Nehemiah, as some of the ablest critics contend, if it does not date back many years earlier, as is not improbable, to say the least of it.

The Book of Ezra, which contains a history of a still earlier period, is equally clear and explicit in its references to the Book of Moses. It is said that they "offered burnt-offering, as it is written in the Law of Moses" (iii., 2); that they "set the priests, . . . as it is written in the Book of Moses" (vi., 18). We read that Ezra was a "ready scribe in the Law of Moses," and that he "prepared his heart to seek the Law of the Lord" (vii., 6, 10). Strange wives are said to have been put away, according to "The Law" (x., 3). This Ezra, a learned scribe in "The Law," is said, in the history which gives an account of his deeds, to have instructed the people in the Law, and to have established the worship as required by the Law. He is evidently fully honored in the book; but the greatest work which *tradition* attributes to him is not alluded to, not hinted at in the most remote manner. I refer to the work of recovering the Law, and putting in order its commands, after they had been lost during the captivity. Of this work, nothing is said, nothing is hinted. "The Book of the Law" is spoken of as something in existence, not as something which Ezra composed or compiled or found. Whatever may have been its origin, Ezra was not its author. And, should there be no evidence of its existence before the time of Ezra or before the captivity, it would still be true that we have not a shadow of historical evidence that Ezra was the author of the book, but, rather, most abundant evidence should we have to the contrary. The quotations which are made from this "Book of the Law" are taken from the Pentateuch as we now have it; and the historical proof is strong that he read to the people the book which has come down to us. So far, the historical notices of the book are all that could be expected under the circumstances. No work of so high antiquity has come down to us with so good evidence of its genuineness.

SECTION III. FROM THE CAPTIVITY TO DAVID.

A broader field now opens before us, and more difficult to traverse. Are there any traces of the existence of this book at an earlier period? Are there any references to such a work in the earlier writings of the Jewish nation, or in writings of the period of Ezra which relate to the earlier times of the people? This is the question which is now to be answered.

Before proceeding to answer the question proposed, however, it is necessary to notice a few particulars touching the writings which have come down to us. They may be divided into two classes, the poetical and the historical. Respecting the latter class, little or nothing need be said by way of explanation. In poetical books, we do not expect such explicit references to books, especially to those which are familiar to us, as in prose compositions. How few references to the New Testament of such a nature as you will see in a librarian's catalogue, or a critic's treatise, will you find in all the poetical works in the English language! Even in our sacred poetry, no such specific titles of the New Testament are found. "God in the gospel of his Son" is, I think, the most specific reference in one of our hymn-books. And, even in sermons, it is not often that book and chapter and verse are referred to. It is sufficient for our purpose, if there is such a reference or allusion to the Gospels as enables us to perceive that such is the poet's or preacher's intent. So in the poetical books of the period preceding and during the captivity. All that we can expect to find, and all that we need to find, to prove the existence of the "Book of the Law," which Ezra read and taught, is such allusion to its contents and spirit, and such use of its words and phrases, as to show that it was in the poet's mind. If we demand more proof than this, we demand what, from the very nature of the case, we ought not to expect.

Respecting the historical books, it should be remembered that a period of probably one thousand years is covered by the Books of Judges, Samuel, and Kings, the whole contents of which would not make a volume larger than the fifth volume of Bancroft's *History of the United States*, which embraces a period of but three years. The Books of Chronicles cover a portion of the same period, beginning with David, and giving only brief genealogies of what preceded his time. Surely, if "The Law" was really a well-known book, we should expect to find but very few specific references to it in these writings. None, indeed, should we expect to find there, unless something very closely connected with the book itself should call for them. All that we can expect is such a reference to manners, customs, institutions, duties, as shall indicate an existing, fundamental law, such as was contained in Ezra's "Book of the Law," which he read to the people, and taught them to obey, as having been given by Moses in conformity to the divine command. More reference than this to the Pentateuch, I hesitate not to say, cannot be expected in these books. Were there more, I should not be surprised to find an argument, drawn from their very frequency, against the reliableness of the books themselves, such as is now drawn against the reliableness of Chronicles, because the writer has dwelt at greater length on ecclesiastical affairs than the writer of the Books of the Kings has seen fit to do. Let us bear in mind, then, as we proceed to examine these books, both poetical and historical, that we must not expect more, nor a different kind of, references to the "Book of the Law" than the circumstances of the case authorize. On the supposition that the Pentateuch did exist as early as the time of David, we cannot expect reasonably any more evidence of the fact from these Jewish writings than I have before indicated.

I. *Evidences from the Historical Writings.*—In the first place, I will examine the *historical* writings which treat of the period before the captivity from the time of David; and, as some objection has been raised against the reliableness of the Books of the Chronicles, I will first examine the Books of the Kings. I will mention the passages in which "The Book of the Law" is referred to, and then I will quote those words and phrases which are evidently taken from that book. This division of the evidence seems necessary in order to bring out its force fully. I will then turn to the Books of the Chronicles, and inquire whether there is such an obvious prejudice in the writer's mind respecting this Book of the Law as to make void all his statements in regard to it.

In the Books of the Kings, we find the following references to the Pentateuch. In the time of Josiah, whose reign closed twenty-three years before the captivity, we read (II. Kings xxii.) that Hilkiah, the high priest, "found the Book of the Law in the house of the Lord," which was then undergoing repairs. When the king "heard the words of the Book of the Law, he rent his clothes"; for the people, both under the reign of his father and that of his grandfather for sixty years, had disregarded the Law utterly, having erected idols in the Temple for the people, and having endeavored by the utmost cruelties to exterminate the worship of Jehovah. And in the twenty-third chapter we read that the king "read all the words of this covenant that were written in this book." And he "commanded all the people to keep the passover, as it is written in the book of this covenant." And he "turned to the Lord with all his soul and with all his might, according to all the Law of Moses."

It will be noticed that the same name is given to the book found by Hilkiah which was given to the book which Ezra used in instructing the people. Some difficulties, however, have been started respecting this transaction which demand a moment's notice. It has been asked significantly how it was possible for Josiah to be entirely ignorant of the contents of the Law of Moses. It has always appeared to me that the answer is very easy, when we consider the condition of the kingdom. Manasseh, the grandfather of Josiah, had reigned most wickedly for fifty-five years. He had introduced all the "abominations of the heathen," had "built altars in the house of the Lord," and had built "altars for all the host of heaven in the two courts of the house of the Lord." He also made his son pass through fire, and "dealt with familiar spirits and wizards," and "shed innocent blood very much, till he had filled Jerusalem from one end to the other." And Amon, his son, the father of Josiah, in his short reign of two years, "forsook the Lord and walked in all the way of his fathers." So that for fifty-seven years the Law had been utterly disregarded, and very probably all the copies of the Law on which the wicked kings could lay their hands had been destroyed. Josiah came to the throne when he was a mere child, only eight years of age. When he had reigned eighteen years, as some maintain, or when he was eighteen years of age, and had reigned ten years, as others suppose, he appears to have learned something about the religion of the fathers, and to have commenced repairs on the Temple. The pious Jews would unquestionably try his disposition toward a change from idol worship; and, when it was found that he was disposed to return to the worship of his fathers, a copy of the Law was produced for his examination. It was very probably the Temple copy,— perhaps the autograph of Moses which had been hidden by the priests to keep it from the destroying hands of Manasseh. As Hilkiah expresses no surprise at finding the book, nor Shaphan at its contents, they probably had arranged this matter so as to put this venerable copy into the king's hands. Taking all these circumstances into the account, it is neither wonderful that Josiah was overwhelmed with grief when the book was read, nor that Hilkiah should have brought the book from its hiding-place at this time. It is possible, to take another view, namely, that, in removing the rubbish from the Temple, the lost Mosaic autograph copy of the Law, which was kept in the Temple for sacred purposes, may have been found. At all events, there is nothing in this account which indicates that the book was not in existence before this time, as some have maintained, but quite the contrary; for how could it have been found if it had not existed before the finding? De Wette admits that the book here found is the Pentateuch. These are his words: "The discovery of the Book of the Law in the Temple, under Josiah's reign, about 624 B.C., re-

EVIDENCES FROM THE HISTORICAL WRITINGS. 93

lated in II. Kings xxii., is the first certain trace of the Pentateuch in its present form." That the Pentateuch was "in its present form" in the time of Josiah is sufficiently clear from the historical proof that we have adduced. Whether De Wette is correct or not in saying that it is the "first certain trace of it in its present form" will soon appear.*

In the reign of Hezekiah, who preceded Josiah about one hundred years, we read (II. Kings xvii., 13) that the kingdom of Israel had neglected the covenant "made with the fathers"; and they are exhorted to turn from their evil ways, and to walk "according to all the Law." In the thirty-fourth and thirty-seventh verses, it is stated that the people "fear not the Lord, neither do they after their statutes or after their ordinances or after the Law and commandment which the

---

* It has been objected to this account of the loss and recovery of the roll of the Law that it is so highly improbable as to render it incredible, and furnish evidence of its being a forgery. But the historical scholar will recall cases more wonderful than this. William Bradford's manuscript History of Plymouth Plantation was cited by Prince in 1736, and composed a part of his library deposited in the tower of the Old South Church, Boston, Mass. It was last cited by Governor Hutchinson in 1767. It was lost, though most diligent search was made for it for *eighty years*, when it was found accidentally in England by the Bishop of Oxford, in the Fulham Library, as he was searching for material for his History of the Protestant Episcopal Church in America.

Bradford's Letter-Book MS. was also lost for many years. At last, a portion of it was accidentally found in a grocer's shop in Halifax, N.S., by James Clarke, Esq. These specimens of lost and recovered MSS. in modern times must suffice to show the perfect credibility of this account of Hilkiah. It will not be considered to the point probably to mention that Herculaneum and Pompeii were lost for over sixteen centuries in the heart of Italy. Most certainly, a Hebrew roll might be lost for sixty years in the ruined, desecrated Temple of Jerusalem.

Prof. W. Robertson Smith says, in his lectures on the Old Testament in the Jewish Church, p. 362, "The comparison of Deuteronomy xviii. with II. Kings xxxiii., *et seq.*, effectually disproves the idea of some critics that the Deuteronomic Code was a forgery of the Temple priests or of their head, the high priest Hilkiah."

Lord commanded the children of Jacob"; ... with whom the Lord had made a covenant and charged them, saying, "Ye shall not fear other gods, nor bow yourselves to them, nor serve them (Exodus xx., 5). ... But the statutes and the ordinances and the Law and the commandment which he wrote for you, ye shall observe, since the Lord brought you out of the land of Egypt." The reference here to *a book*, and the *same* book which Josiah found, is too clear to need comment. It is so minutely described as containing the "statutes" and "ordinances" and "commandments" that there seems to be no room for reasonable doubt about the identity of the books. If room for doubt is left by these passages, chapter xviii., 6, closes it: Hezekiah "clave to the Lord, and kept his commandments which the Lord commanded Moses."

In about 830 B.C., a hundred years before the reign of Hezekiah, we read (II. Kings xiv., 6) that Amaziah, King of Judah, "slew not the children of the murderers [who had slain his father], according unto that which is written in the *Book of the Law of Moses*, wherein the Lord commanded, saying, The fathers shall not be put to death for the children, nor the children be put to death for the fathers" (Deuteronomy xxiv., 16). Here the "Book" is distinctly spoken of as having been in existence in the time of Amaziah, two hundred years before the reign of Josiah. If it should be said that this is a remark of the historian derived from the opinions of his own time, the case is varied but little; for it would show that in this time the antiquity of the book was the common belief.

About fifty years earlier than this, when Jehoash was

anointed king, we read (II. Kings xi., 12) that a part of the ceremony of his coronation consisted in giving him "the testimony," or, as De Wette and Gesenius translate, "The Law." In Deuteronomy xvii., 18, 19, it is required of the king that he should have "a copy of the Law," . . . "to read therein all the days of his life." It is also recorded of Jehu, who reigned over Israel but a few years earlier, that he "took no heed to walk in the Law of the Lord God of Israel" (II. Kings x., 31). When the days drew nigh that David should die, he called Solomon to him, and charged him most solemnly to walk in the ways of the Lord, "to keep his statutes and his commandments and his judgments and his testimonies, as it is written in the Law of Moses" (I. Kings ii., 3).

Such are the explicit references in the Books of the Kings to the Law of Moses. The references are made to one book, the same as that which Josiah had, and from which Ezra taught. In about sixty pages of the copy of the Bible before me, containing a civil history of five hundred years, could more specific references to the Pentateuch have been expected? So brief, so limited, is the history that but few facts of any kind could be stated: much less could there be a continual, specific reference by name to a book which was so well known as that which contained the fundamental law of the nation must necessarily have been.

The last remark suggests another argument in favor of the existence of the book during the period of the Kings. It is that the sins rebuked are violations of the Mosaic Law, that the blessings promised are conditional upon obedience to that law. The whole tone of the history is taken from the Pentateuch. I will enter into a more minute examination of this phenomena, that the force of the argument derived from it may be more fully appreciated. This is the second division of the evidence to be derived from the Books of the Kings which I proposed to examine. If we discover that a writer is *borrowing words and phrases* which we find in a book to which he sometimes refers by the usual title, we are still more confirmed in the belief that he had before him the identical book which has come into our hands; just as, when we find the *phraseology* of the New Testament in the sermon or history which we are reading, we feel assured that the author had a copy of that book substantially like our own. I have already, in the examination of the Books of the Kings, made one or two quotations which contain passages from the Pentateuch. *I will now proceed to show that there is a Mosaic phraseology, an introduction and use of religious terms and antique expressions which indicate familiarity with the Books of Moses;* as the phrases, "was let hitherto," "thorn in the flesh," "given to hospitality," indicate familiarity with the language of the New Testament.

In I. Kings ii., 3, Solomon is directed to keep the Law, that "he may prosper in all that he does,"— a verbal quotation from Deuteronomy xxix., 9, except the change of person from plural to singular, to adapt it to the person addressed. In the prayer which Solomon delivered at the dedication of the Temple, there are numerous words and phrases taken from the Pentateuch, such as, "if any man trespass against his neighbor," "blasting and mildew," "the people of thine inheritance," "the Lord is God, there is none else." And if we consider that, in connection with the use of these phrases, Solomon makes use of thes expressions, "*as thou spakest by the hand of Moses thy servant*, when thou broughtest our fathers out of the land of Egypt," "there hath not failed one word of all his good promise *which he promised by the hand of Moses his servant*," we cannot but feel a strong assurance, not to say certainty, that we have the book which contained those promises. In chapter xxi., 3, Naboth says to Ahab, who had proposed that Naboth should give him his vineyard, "The Lord forbid it me that I should give the inheritance of my fathers unto thee." The "inheritance of the fathers" was inalienable according to the Law, and was considered very precious, as may be seen by referring to Numbers xxxvi. In chapter xxii., 11, Zedekiah, a false prophet, who had "made him horns of iron," declared to Ahab, "With these shalt thou push the Syrians," referring directly to Deuteronomy xxxiii., 17, where it is said of Joseph, "His horns are like the horns of unicorns; with them shall he push the people together to the ends of the earth." In the seventeenth verse of the same chapter, it is said, "I saw all Israel ... as sheep that have not a shepherd." This phrase is taken from Numbers xxvii., 17: "That the congregation of the Lord be not as sheep which have no shepherd." The agreement in the Hebrew is verbal. In the twenty-seventh verse, a prophet is sentenced by the king to eat the "bread of affliction," a phrase taken from Deuteronomy xvi., 3, where the poor bread which the people were compelled to eat on their departure from Egypt is so called. In II. Kings ii., 9, Elisha prays Elijah, "Let a double portion of thy spirit rest on me." This phrase, "double portion," is taken from Deuteronomy xxi., 17, where the portion of the "first-born" is described and defined. The use of the word *phé* in the sense of "portion" is found but three times in the Old Testament. In chapter iii., 19, 20, we find Elisha directing the king, when he made war upon the Moabites, to "fell every good tree," which is an allusion to Deuteronomy xx., 19, 20. In chapter iv., 16, we find a very peculiar expression relating to the birth of a child which is also found in Genesis xviii., 10, 14, where Sarah is assured that she shall have a son. The similarity of the two cases in some of their circumstances no doubt prompted the use of the peculiar phrase in Kings, "About this season, according to the time of life, thou shalt embrace a son." In the forty-second verse of this chapter, we read that a man brought to Elisha "bread of the first-fruits, twenty loaves of barley, and full ears of corn" (*carmel*). This word is used to denote the "polenta of early grain in Leviticus ii., 14; xxiii., 14," says Gesenius. In chapter v., 27, we read that the servant of Elisha went out from his presence "a leper white as snow." This peculiar phrase is used in Numbers xii., 10; Exodus iv., 6; and nowhere else. The phrase as used in those passages under such peculiar circumstances is very strongly marked, and is used by the writer in Kings to indicate the severity of the punishment which fell upon the servant of Elisha. A peculiar word is used in Genesis xix., 11, to indicate blindness: "They smote the men that were at the door with blindness." This Hebrew word is used in II. Kings vi., 18: "Smite, I pray thee, this people with blindness." Elisha doubtless had in his mind the peculiar word which indicated the blindness with which the rioters about Lot's house had been smitten. The word is used in only these two instances. In chapter vii., 2, an unbeliever is represented as addressing Elisha thus: "If the Lord would make windows in heaven, might this thing be?" In Genesis vii., 11, "the windows of heaven" are spoken of as having been opened to produce the devastating flood. So here the speaker says that, when a flood comes again, this which you have predicted may happen. So references in the Prophets are made to the same event in this peculiar phrase (Isaiah xxiv., 18; Malachi iii., 10), which is used nowhere else.

Such is a specimen of the peculiar words which are used in the Books of the Kings, taken from the Pentateuch. But we also find in these books statements respecting the observance of ordinances required in the Pentateuch. In I. Kings xviii., 29, 36, we read of the "time of offering the evening sacrifice," as required in Exodus xxix., 39; and in II. Kings iii., 20, we read that aid was afforded "in the morning when the meat offering was offered." Compare this with the same passage in Exodus, and we shall find that offerings were required morning and evening, and that a meat (or meal) offering was to be offered with the lamb. In II. Kings iv., 23, we read of two festal days, "the new moon" and "the Sabbath." And, in the first verse of the same chapter, we read of a creditor of whom a woman says, he "is come to take unto him my two sons to be bondmen." This the Law (Leviticus xxv., 39) permitted and regulated. Solomon is represented as "offering burnt-offerings and peace-offerings," both of which were required by the Law. He also assembled all the people "at the feast in the month Ethanim, which is the seventh month." This was the feast of the tabernacle, and the Temple was dedicated at this time. On account of the joyfulness of the occasion, Solomon doubled the days of this most joyful of all the feasts. In I. Kings xii., 32, after the division of the kingdom, we read that Jeroboam "ordained a feast in the eighth month, on the fifteenth day of the month, like unto the feast that is in Judah, . . . in a month which he had devised of his own heart." Well did the historian say this, for the Law required the feast to be in the seventh month, not in the eighth.

The testimony rendered in the Books of the Kings — by the name of the book, by the use of its peculiar terms, by the quotations made from its contents, by the description of observances, sacrifices, feasts, offerings, such as the Law requires — to the existence of "the Book of the Law of Moses" which Ezra used in teaching the people is as full and as specific as, under the circumstances, we could expect. Had we no other writings of this period, the proof of the existence of the Pentateuch would be as great as that which is furnished for the antiquity of any other work of that age. But there are other writings. The Books of the Chronicles are still to be examined.

The writer of these Books of the Chronicles speaks more of ecclesiastical affairs, and hence we would expect to find in his writings more frequent reference to the rites and ceremonies of their religion. De Wette, Kuenen especially, and others, have decried these books because they have what they call a Levitical spirit. I am not sure that a priestly spirit is more likely to bias an historian than a political spirit. There has been no evidence brought that the bias of the writer has corrupted his integrity. At all events, I am sure that the reader, after comparing what the chronicler has recorded respecting the Law with what is said respecting it in the Books of the Kings, will not be disposed to think that his Levitical bias has done him serious harm as an historian. Let us, then, see what this writer, who has been so unceremoniously treated, has to say of the Law, and the customs of the people so far as they regarded the Law.

In I. Chronicles xvi., 40, we read that Zadok the priest did "according to all that is written in the Law of the Lord, which he commanded Israel." In chapter xxii., 12, 13, David charges Solomon to "keep the Law of the Lord," and to "take heed to fulfil the statutes and judgments which the Lord charged Moses with concerning Israel." In II. Chronicles vi., 16, Solomon prays that God's promise to his father, founded on this condition,— if "thy children take heed to walk in my Law,"— may be fulfilled in him. This passage has been quoted before, from Kings. In chapter xii., 1, Rehoboam is said to have forsaken "the Law of the Lord." In chapter xiv., 4, Judah is commanded "to do the Law." In chapter xvii. is an account of the good king Jehoshaphat's sending out teachers to instruct the people ; and "*they took the Book of the Law of the Lord with them*, and went about throughout all the cities of Judah, and taught the people." In chapter xxiii., 18, it is said that Jehoiada appointed persons who should "offer the burnt-offerings of the Lord, *as it is written in the Law of Moses.*" In chapter xxv., 4, we read that Amaziah slew not the children of his father's murderers, "but did as it is written in *the Law of the Book of Moses*, where the Lord commanded, saying, "The fathers shall not die for the children, neither shall the children die for the fathers, but every man shall die for his own sin." This passage is quoted from Deuteronomy xxiv., 16. The parallel passage is II. Kings xiv., 6. In chapter xxx., 16, we read that the priests and Levites stood in their "place, ... according to the Law of Moses." In the thirty-first chapter, Hezekiah directs that "morning and evening burnt-offerings, and the burnt-offerings for the Sabbaths, and for the new moons, and for the set feasts" shall be offered, "as it is written in the Law of the Lord." He further directed that "the portion of the priests and Levites" should be given them, "that they might be encouraged in the Law of the Lord." And "every work that he began ... in the Law ... he did with all his heart." In chapter xxxiii., 8, we read of "the whole Law and statutes and ordinances *by the hand of Moses.*" In chapter xxxiv., we have an account of the finding of the "Book of the Law of the Lord given by Moses," parallel to the passage in II. Kings xxii. In chapter xxxv., Josiah commands to kill the passover "according to the word of the Lord by the hand of Moses"; and they did "*as it is written in the Book of Moses.*" And the good king's acts were "according to that which was written in the Law of the Lord." It will be observed that the "Book of Moses" and "the Law of the Lord" are identical.

Such is the manner in which the Pentateuch is spoken

of in the Books of the Chronicles. There is no marked difference between the style of reference and that in the Kings. Nor are the references much more numerous. These *titles* of the book, or the *names* by which it is called, are the same as those which we found in the Books of the Kings, in Ezra, in Nehemiah, in Malachi, in Ecclesiasticus, and in Maccabees. The same names being used, the inference is that the same book is referred to. But as we found quotations from the book in Kings, so we do in the Chronicles, still more certainly identifying it as the same book by its contents. The use of peculiar and emphatic terms which are found in the Pentateuch shows that the writer was familiar with the book as we now have it. The people are exhorted not to be "stiff-necked" as their fathers were,—II. Chronicles xxx., 8. In the Pentateuch, this is a favorite term. "The mighty hand and stretched-out arm" are spoken of in chapter vi., 32, which is a peculiar phrase of the Pentateuch. God is said to be "gracious and merciful," chapter xxx., 9, which is a quotation from Exodus xxxiv., 6. It is used elsewhere in the Pentateuch, however. In chapter xxx., 15, we read that "they killed the passover on the fourteenth day of the second month"; and "kept the feast of unleavened bread seven days," verse 21. This is in accordance with what is recorded in Exodus xii. The feasts are spoken of. In chapter viii., 13, we read of the solemn feasts, three times a year, "even the feast of unleavened bread, and the feast of weeks, and the feast of tabernacles." And in these books, as in the Books of the Kings, the whole tone of rebuke and approbation is taken from the standard established in the Pentateuch.

Nothing could be expected different in their style and tone, if it were mathematically certain that the Pentateuch existed at this time, by information derived from an entirely different source.

I have now examined the historical works which treat of the condition of the people from the time of David. It is for the reader to determine whether there is not as much and as explicit reference to the Pentateuch as, under the circumstances, could be expected. What book of that age can be so certainly traced in history? We have found no hint of any remodelling of the work, and we have no historical reason to suppose that any such thing was done. Without any farther evidence, we have sufficient proof of the existence of the Pentateuch in the days of David, within three or four centuries of the time of Moses. But the whole field of the poetical books is yet to be explored. Further and striking evidence will here appear of the antiquity of the "Law of Moses, the man of God."

II. *Evidence from the Poetical Books.*—I have already remarked that in poetical works we do not expect to find books referred to by quoting their title-page; and usually we may expect that the reference will be the less explicit as the work referred to is well known. We shall only look for general terms and phrases, and shall often expect to find some word expressive of the contents of the book used by metonymy to denote the book itself. In the historical books, we have found that the Pentateuch was referred to by the name of "The Law," "The Law of Moses," "The Law of the Lord," "The statutes, judgments, commandments, and ordinances of the Lord." We may therefore expect to find only these, and still more general, names given to the book by the poets.

1. The Book of Daniel is supposed by many to have been written at a late period, long after the captivity. As I do not propose to enter into any discussion respecting the age of the books which I shall quote, I will only remark that, if Daniel was written at as late a period as is maintained by some, it shows how the Pentateuch was referred to at that time, and enables us to trace the book, by the manner in which it is spoken of, back to earlier times. In Daniel ix., 10, 11, 13, we find the prophet lamenting, in his prayer, the sins of the people; and he confesses as follows: "Neither have we obeyed the voice of the Lord our God to walk in his laws.... Yea, all Israel have transgressed thy Law;... and therefore the curse is poured upon us... that is written in the Law of Moses, the servant of God.... And he hath confirmed his words,... as it is written in the Law of Moses." That the Pentateuch is here referred to is past all question.

2. Habakkuk, speaking of the violence that prevailed in the land, gives, as a reason for it, that "the Law is slacked, and judgment doth never go forth," chapter i., 4.

3. Zephaniah, chapter ii., 3, exhorts all those "to seek the Lord which have wrought his judgment," *i.e.*, obeyed his Law; for we shall soon find that this word sometimes stands for the whole Law.

4. Ezekiel, who lived during the captivity, prophesying of the evil yet to befall the people, says, chapter vii., 26, "The Law shall perish from the priests." In

the name of God, he says to the people, chapter v., 6, "they have refused my judgments and my statutes, and have not walked in them." He declares, chapter xi., 20, that their heart will yet become flesh, so that they will walk in "the statutes and keep the ordinances" of the Lord. He repeats the same truth in chapter xxxvi., 27. In the eighteenth chapter, the same expressions are used to denote the Law; and specific statutes are referred to. He promises that blessings shall attend the man who "hath not defiled his neighbor's wife" (Leviticus xviii., 20); nor hath come near to a woman when she is ritually unclean,—a technical term (Leviticus xviii., 19); nor hath "oppressed any" (Leviticus xxv., 14); "but hath restored to the debtor his pledge" (Exodus xxii., 26); "hath spoiled none by violence" (Leviticus vi., 2); "hath given his bread to the needy, and hath covered the naked with a garment" (Deuteronomy xv., 7, 8); that "hath not given forth upon usury" (Exodus xxii., 25); that "hath executed true judgment between man and man" (Leviticus xix., 15). In chapter xi., 12, Ezekiel gives as a reason why so great punishments should fall upon these people that they "have not walked in the statutes nor executed the judgments" of the Lord, but have done after the manner of the heathen. If we look into the Law (Leviticus xviii., 4, 5), we shall find it declared that the people shall not do according to other people's laws and customs; and it is commanded them, "Ye shall keep my statutes and my judgments." These references will suffice for this prophet, to show that he quotes the Law, and that he gives it the same names, in his references to it, which are given by other writers whose works we have examined.*

5. From Ezekiel, I will pass to Jeremiah, who was his contemporary for a part of his life. Jeremiah went from Jerusalem into Egypt. Ezekiel, many years previ-

* "It is difficult," says a writer in *The Unitarian Review* for November, 1880, p. 431, "it is difficult to read his [Ezekiel's] pages written in Babylon, and believe that any important priestly legislation had preceded them. He does not quote from existing laws." In view of this unqualified denial from so respectable a source, I feel called upon to invite the reader's attention to farther proof that Ezekiel's writings give *overwhelming* evidence of his acquaintance with "existing laws." It is assumed from the character of the writer that no quibble is intended in the use of the word "quote." If it is meant that the name of the writer, and the chapter and verse in which the quotation may be found, are not mentioned, then there is an instant end to the discussion. But, if it is meant that there are no clear quotations of statutes and phrases from the Pentateuch as definitely made as could be expected in a poetical address, then I must take direct issue, and appeal to the judgment of the reader by fortifying my previous references; and the reader is especially requested to observe that the captivity of the people is ascribed to disobeying the law quoted.

Examples: Ezekiel iv., 14, "Behold, my soul hath not been polluted; for I have not eaten of that which dieth of itself, or is torn in pieces; neither came there abominable flesh into my mouth." Compare now the different laws on this subject: Exodus xxii., 31, "Neither shall ye eat any flesh that is torn of beasts"; Leviticus xvii., 15, "And he shall be unclean until the even"; Deuteronomy xiv., 3, "Thou shalt not eat any abominable thing"; and Leviticus xxii., 8, "That which dieth of itself, or is torn, he shall not eat." These scattered laws are condensed by Ezekiel. Ezekiel iv., 16, reads, "I will break the staff of bread in Jerusalem; and they shall eat bread by weight, and with care"; Leviticus xxvi., 26, "When I have broken the staff of your bread, . . . they shall deliver you your bread by weight"; Ezekiel v., 10, "The fathers shall eat the sons in the midst of thee, and the sons shall eat their fathers, . . . and the whole remnant of thee will I scatter into all the winds." Compare Leviticus xxvi., 29, "And ye shall eat the flesh of your sons, and the flesh of your daughters"; and verse 33, "And I will scatter you among the heathen"; also Deuteronomy xxviii., 64, "The Lord shall scatter thee among all people, from the one end of the earth even unto the other." This is another instance of Ezekiel's condensing separate threatenings into one. Ezekiel v., 12, "I will scatter a third part into all the winds, and I will draw out a sword after them"; Leviticus xxvi., 33, "I will scatter you among the heathen, and will draw out a sword after you"; Ezekiel xiv., 14, 15, "I will make thee waste, and a reproach among the nations. . . . It shall be a reproach and a taunt, an instruction and an astonishment unto the nations"; Leviticus xxvi., 31, "I will make your cities waste, and bring your sanctuaries unto desolation, . . . and your ene-

ously, went to Babylonia as a captive. The following remarkable quotation from the Pentateuch is found in Jeremiah iv., 23, "I beheld the earth, and, lo, it was *without form and void,*" a phrase found only in Genesis i., 2. In chapter ii., 8, the prophet says, in the

mies . . . shall be astonished at it." So Deuteronomy xxviii., 37, "Thou shalt become an astonishment, a proverb, and a by-word among all nations"; Ezekiel v., 17, "I will send upon you famine, and evil beasts, and they shall bereave thee"; Leviticus xxvi., 22, "I will also send wild beasts among you, which shall rob you of your children"; Ezekiel vi., 4, 5, "I will destroy your high places, your altars shall be desolate and your images shall be broken, and I will cast down your slain before your idols, and I will lay the dead carcasses of the children of Israel before their idols"; Leviticus xxvi., 30, "I will destroy your high places and cut down your images, and cast your carcasses upon the carcasses of your idols"; Ezekiel vi., 6, "The cities shall be laid waste, and the high places shall be desolate"; Leviticus xxvi., 31, "I will make your cities waste, and bring your sanctuaries unto desolation"; Ezekiel xiv., 8, "I will set my face against that man, . . . and will cut him off from the midst of my people"; Leviticus xvii., 10, "I will set my face against that soul, . . . and will cut him off from among his people"; Ezekiel xiv., 15, "Wild beasts will desolate the land." So Leviticus xxvi., 22; Ezekiel xvi., 59, "Thou hast despised the oath in breaking the covenant"; Deuteronomy xxix., 12, "That thou shouldest enter into covenant with the Lord thy God, and into his oath"; verse 14, "Neither with you only do I make this covenant and this oath"; Ezekiel xviii., 6. There is a special reference to the law respecting the relation of the sexes, which is found in Leviticus xviii., 19, 20, and xxiv., 18; Ezekiel xviii., 7, "And hath not oppressed any, but hath restored to the debtor his pledge"; Exodus xxii., 26, "If thou take thy neighbor's raiment to pledge, thou shalt deliver it to him by that the sun goeth down"; xxiii., 9, "Thou shalt not oppress a stranger"; Ezekiel xviii., 20, "The son shall not bear the iniquity of the father, neither shall the father bear the iniquity of the son"; Deuteronomy xxiv., 16, "The fathers shall not be put to death for the children, neither shall the children be put to death for the fathers"; Ezekiel xx., 6, "a land flowing with milk and honey"; Exodus iii., 8, "a good land, . . . a land flowing with milk and honey"; Ezekiel xx., 11, "And I gave them my statutes, and showed them my judgments, which if a man do he shall live in them"; Leviticus xviii., 5, "Ye shall keep my statutes and my judgments, which if a man do he shall live in them"; Ezekiel xx., 12, "I gave them my sabbaths, to be a sign between me and them"; Exodus xxxi., 13, "My sabbaths ye shall keep, for it is a sign between me and you"; Ezekiel xx., 13, "Then I said, I would pour out my fury upon them in the wilderness, to consume them"; Numbers xiv., 29, 32, 33, "So will I do to you: your carcasses shall fall in this wilderness"; Ezekiel xx., 23, "I lifted up my hand unto them also in the wilderness, that I would scatter them among the heathen, and

name of the Lord, "They that handle the Law knew me not"; for the priests and the prophets whose office it was to know the Law were both of them violating it by serving Baal. In chapter xviii., 8, the prophet complains, in a prayer to the Lord, of the boasting of

disperse them through the countries." The threatening is recorded in Leviticus xxvi., 33, "I will scatter you among the heathen"; Ezekiel xx., 31, "When ye offer your gifts, when ye make your sons to pass through the fire"; Leviticus xviii., 21, "Thou shalt not let any of thy seed pass through the fire to Molech." This chapter is largely the language of the Levitical law: Ezekiel xxii., 7, "They have set light by father and mother"; Deuteronomy xxvii., 16, "Cursed be he that setteth light by his father or his mother"; also, "They have dealt oppression with the stranger"; Exodus xxii., 21, "Thou shalt neither vex a stranger, nor oppress him"; also, "In thee have they vexed the fatherless and the widow"; Exodus xxii., 22, "Ye shall not afflict any widow or fatherless child." In Ezekiel xxii., the language and phrases and sentences of the Pentateuch are so frequent as to forbid quotation. After one more quotation, I must refer the interested reader to the chapter itself. Verse 26 reads thus: "Her priests have violated my law, and have profaned mine holy things: they have put no difference between the holy and profane, neither have they showed difference between the unclean and the clean, and have hid their eyes from my sabbaths, and I am profaned among them"; Leviticus xxii., 2, "Speak unto Aaron and to his sons, ... that they profane not my holy name in those things which they hallow unto me"; x., 10, "And that ye put difference between holy and unholy, and between unclean and clean." Here is certainly a clear reference to priests, to a ritual law, and the duty of observing it. There are not less than twenty distinct references to the law and passages from it in this chapter of only thirty-one verses.

It would seem to most minds a sheer waste of time and patience to pursue this inquiry further, but one or two more passages demand attention: Ezekiel xxiv., 7, "Her blood, ... she poured it not upon the ground to cover it with dust"; Leviticus xvii., 13, "He shall even pour out the blood thereof, and cover it with dust." In Deuteronomy xii., 16, it reads, "Ye shall pour out the blood upon the earth as water," and nothing is said of "covering it with dust," showing that Ezekiel had the priestly law of Leviticus before him, or in mind, which, according to Kuenen's hypothesis, was not written till a century after his death! If the reader has interest enough to do it, and is not yet satisfied, he may compare Ezekiel xxviii., 24, with Numbers xxxiii., 55; and Ezekiel xxxiii., 15, with Exodus xxii., 4, Numbers v., 6, Leviticus xviii., 5; and Ezekiel xxxiii., 25, with Leviticus vii., 26; Ezekiel xxxiv., 25-27, with Leviticus xxvi., 6, 7; Ezekiel xxxvi., 3, 17, with Deuteronomy xxviii., 37, Leviticus xviii., 25; and Ezekiel xxxix., 23, with Deuteronomy xxxi., 17. But enough: I must hold my hand.

I have taken pains to compare the frequency of Ezekiel's use of the language

the wicked, who say, "The Law shall not perish from the priest." In chapter xliv., 23, he upbraids the people because they have not "obeyed the voice of the Lord, nor walked in his Law, nor in his statutes, nor in his testimonies." And in the tenth verse he is still more explicit: speaking in the name of the Lord, he says, "Ye have not walked in my Law, nor in my statutes that I set before you and before *your fathers*." In the twenty-second verse, he says that on account of their sins their "land is a desolation and an astonishment and a curse,"— words used in Leviticus xxvi., 32, to denote the punishment which should follow transgression. These are a specimen of the terms used by this prophet when he refers to the Pentateuch. The whole spirit and almost letter of Jeremiah's prophesy is based upon the Pentateuch. His promises and threatenings are all founded upon the laws therein contained. All the rites and ceremonies which he describes are such as are found in "The Law." There is but one passage which appears to invalidate this

in the law, and references to it and quotations from it, with that of four of our most celebrated preachers' reference to the gospel, or quotations from it. Dr. Dewey, in the *Two Great Commandments*, a volume of three hundred pages, uses the language of the Gospels (texts of sermons excepted) but *forty-five* times. Mr. Martineau, in *Hours of Thought* second series, uses the language of the Gospels *twenty-five* times. Dr. Channing, in the *Perfect Life*, uses the language of the Gospels *eight* times in two hundred pages. Dr. Walker, in *Reason, Faith, and Duty*, uses the language of the Gospels *eighteen* times in two hundred pages; and in but *two* instances does he say he takes it from the Gospels, and in but very few instances do the others.

Since this note was written, I learn (*Bibliotheca Sacra*, April, 1881, p. 390) that Prof. R. Smend, in his recent work, *The Prophet Ezekiel* (*Der Prophet Ezechiel*), 1880, maintains that the Levitical law was developed from Ezekiel, and not Ezekiel's quotations taken from the law. Of any such hypothesis, the reading of Ezekiel is the swiftest and most conclusive confutation. Ezekiel's quotations are not only from a law *already* in existence, but from a law *given to the fathers*, and for *not obeying which* they were carried captive.

conclusion. It is contained in chapter vii., 21-23: "Put your burnt-offerings unto your sacrifices, and eat flesh. For I spake not unto your fathers, nor commanded them in the day that I brought them out of the land of Egypt, concerning burnt-offerings or sacrifices. But this thing commanded I them, saying, Obey my voice and I will be your God, and ye shall be my people." The state of mind in which the prophet uttered this passage must be considered, in order to understand his meaning. "The children gather wood," says he, "and the fathers kindle the fire, and the women knead their dough to make cakes to the queen of heaven, and to pour out drink-offerings unto other gods," in the streets of Jerusalem. The flagrant violation of the Law in offering these sacrifices to such vile gods in the streets of the city so fired his soul with indignation that he put the comparative value of sacrifices and an obedient heart in direct contrast with each other: "The Lord did not command sacrifices; he required a pure heart." Another view is that the prophet here made a sharp distinction between what was commanded and what was only regulated. It is contended by some critics that sacrifices are regulated by the Law, not commanded by it,—they were already in existence, like circumcision.* Whatever view we may take of the prophet's meaning, we cannot understand him as looking upon sacrifices as offensive to God; for in chapter xvii., 26, in describing the great glory and pure worship of the blessed period which would come after their enemies were destroyed and God's kingdom

---

* Leviticus i., 2., "Speak unto the children of Israel and say unto them, *if* any man bring an offering unto the LORD, ye shall bring," etc.

was established, he says, "They shall come from the cities of Judah, and from the places about Jerusalem, and from the land of Benjamin, and from the plain, and from the mountains, and from the south, bringing burnt-offerings and sacrifices and meat-offerings and incense, and bringing sacrifices of praise unto the house of the Lord." The more probable interpretation is that which is founded upon the supposition that the prophet is asserting a strong negative to show the comparative value of sacrifices and the spirit in which they should be offered. But, admitting that we could adopt no interpretation which would reconcile this passage with others, it would not be reasonable to deny the assertion of a hundred passages because of the apparent counter assertion of one. His prophecy teaches most clearly that offering sacrifices in accordance with the regulations of the Pentateuch was a part of the national worship, and shows, whatever was the origin of that book, that it was in existence in his time. This, indeed, is the only point which I am now endeavoring to establish. In Lamentations, it is said, chap. ii., 9, that "the Law is no more"; that is, not regarded.

6. Passing now to a still earlier period, we come to Isaiah who flourished about 730 B.C. The style of his poetry is much loftier than that of the prophets whom we have examined, and hence we should expect to find fewer explicit references to the statute-book of the nation. I do not speak too strongly, however, when I say that the prophecies of Isaiah are based upon the doctrines of the Pentateuch. Their tone and spirit are just as we should expect them to be, if Isaiah had made himself familiar with that book. In describ-

ing the future glory of the kingdom, in a passage taken from a still earlier prophet, he says, "For out of Zion shall go forth *the Law*," to be established among all nations. In the eighth chapter, he rebukes the people for going after false gods, "and to wizards that peep and mutter"; and asks, "Should not a people seek unto their own God? ... To *the Law* and to the testimony; if they speak not according to this word, it is because there is no light in them." Nothing can be clearer than that the prophet counsels the people to study the book of their own law instead of consulting wizards, if they wish to learn their duty. In chapter xlii., 21, 24, the prophet declares that, notwithstanding the neglect which it has received, the Lord "will magnify the Law and make it honorable"; and he gives as a reason why Jacob had been given for a spoil and Israel to robbers, that they "would not walk in the ways of the Lord, neither were obedient to his Law." Gesenius says that the phrase, "I will make my judgment to rest for a light of the people" (chap. li., 4), refers to the Mosaic Law. It should be remarked concerning the last two passages that they are in that portion of Isaiah which has been assigned to a later date and another writer. In chapter xxiv., 5, it is affirmed that the people "have transgressed the laws, changed the ordinance, and broken the everlasting covenant." By these terms "The Law" is referred to in other books, and very probably they refer to it here. In the first chapter of his prophecy, Isaiah rebukes severely those who "trample the courts of the Lord," bringing their sacrifice with wicked hearts and bloody hands. He says to the people, if "ye be willing and obedient, ye shall eat of the good of the land." This is in conformity with the Law, Deuteronomy iv., 30; viii., 20; and many other places. He speaks of their "new moons" and "appointed feasts." He asks where the people can be "smitten" again, since "from the sole of the foot even unto the head there is no soundness in it," with evident reference to Deuteronomy xxviii., 35, where it is said of the nation, if it sin, "The Lord shall smite thee . . . with a sore botch that cannot be healed, from the sole of thy foot to the top of thy head." He says to them, "Your country is desolate; your cities are burned with fire; your land — strangers devour it, and it is desolate," as it was foretold would be the case in Deuteronomy xxviii., where it is said, "The nation from far . . . shall eat the fruit of thy land" until it be "destroyed." "But," he continues, "if ye be willing and be obedient, ye shall consume the good of the land; but, if ye refuse and rebel, ye shall be devoured with the sword; for the mouth of the Lord hath spoken it." In Leviticus xxvi., 5, the Lord says, "If ye walk in my statutes, . . . ye shall eat your bread to the full"; but, if ye will not hearken to me, I "will draw out a sword after you" (verse 33); "my sword shall devour flesh" (Deuteronomy xxxii., 42). In the description which the prophet gives of the enemy which he will call to destroy his wicked people, there is evident allusion to Deuteronomy xxviii., 49, 50. Isaiah says (chap. v., 26, 27), "He will lift up an ensign to the nations from far, and will hiss them from the end of the earth. . . . They shall come with speed swiftly." In Deuteronomy, referred to above, Moses says, "The Lord shall bring a nation against thee from far, from the end of the earth, as swift as an eagle flieth." These specimens must suffice to show how Isaiah's style abounds with words and phrases which are taken from the Pentateuch. They prove that the style of the old Law Book and its very words were imbedded in his mind so as to make a part of his thoughts.

7. The prophet Micah was a contemporary of Isaiah. His short prophecy is based, in all its rebukes and promises, upon the laws and threatenings and promises made in the Pentateuch. In the closing verse of his prophecy, he declares that faithfulness and mercy will yet visit the people, "which," he says, addressing the Lord, "thou hast sworn unto our fathers from the days of old." These promises will be found in Genesis xii., 2; xxvi., 24; xxviii., 13; Deuteronomy xxx., 1–5. I will not pause to examine minutely this prophecy. It exhibits the same characteristics as does that of Isaiah; and, as he was contemporary with that prophet, it is less important to present his allusions, mostly quite obscure, to the Law. And I pass on the more readily, since Dr. Kuenen, in his elaborate work on *The Religion of Israel*, admits that the references of Micah are so numerous and so exact to the events recorded in the Pentateuch that "we must even suppose that he was acquainted with those narratives, unless appearances should tend to show that they were written or modified at a later date" (Vol. I., p. 103). I will therefore proceed to a consideration of the prophecies of Hosea, Amos, and Joel, taking them up in order.

8. Hosea (780 B.C.) says to the people (chap. iv., 6), "Thou hast forgotten the Law of thy God." Again, he says (chap. viii., 1), "They have transgressed my

covenant and trespassed against my Law," therefore "He shall come as an eagle against the house of the Lord." The reference is to Deuteronomy xxviii., 49, "The Lord shall bring a nation . . . as swift as an eagle flieth." Speaking of Ephraim, in the name of the Lord, he says (viii., 12), "I have written to him the great things of my Law, but they were counted as a strange thing." One of the distinguishing features of the style of this book is the repeated use of the words "whore," "whoring," "whoredom," to signify desertion of the true God and worship of false gods. This phraseology is derived from the Pentateuch most obviously. In Exodus xxxiv., 15, 16; Leviticus xx., 5, 6; Numbers xiv., 33; Deuteronomy xxxi., 16, and in numerous other places, these words are used to signify idolatry. Indeed, the style of Hosea is colored *through and through* with the style of the Books of Moses. I will commence with the first chapter and proceed with an examination of his style as far as is necessary for my purpose. The land is said (chap. i., 2) to have "committed a great whoredom." Leviticus xix., 29, "Lest the land fall to ["commit"; the original word is the same as in Hosea] whoredom." In verse 10, it is said, "The number of the children of Israel shall be as the sand of the sea, which cannot be measured nor numbered," which is a verbal quotation from the promise made to Jacob (Genesis xxxii., 12), "I will make thy seed as the sand of the sea, which cannot be numbered for multitude." In the eleventh verse, the prophet says that the people "shall come up out of the land" of their captivity. This phrase is used repeatedly in the Pentateuch when the deliverance from

Egypt is spoken of, and therefore had great significance to the Jews. In chapter ii, 8, the prophet says, "She," Israel, "did not know that I gave her corn and wine and oil," a quotation from Deuteronomy vii., 13, where God says, "I will bless the fruit of thy land, thy corn and thy wine and thine oil." And, in the tenth verse, God says, "None shall deliver her out of my hand," a phrase taken from Deuteronomy xxxii., 39, "Neither is there any that can deliver out of my hand." In verse 11, we have mention of "her feast days," which are the Passover, Pentecost, and Tabernacles; her "new moons," Numbers xxviii., 11, 12; and "her Sabbaths," Leviticus xxiii., 3; "and all her solemn feasts." A very clear reference is made in the twelfth verse, in the word "rewards," meaning wages of whoredom, to Deuteronomy xxiii, 18. It is said in verse 17 that the Lord would take the "names of Baalim out of her mouth," which phrase is used in Exodus xxiii., 13, "make no mention of the names of other gods, neither let it be heard out of thy mouth." In chapter iv., 4, we read that reproof and rebuke are useless, for the "people are as they that strive with the priest." And how were they that strove with the priest? In Deuteronomy xvii., 12, we read that the "man that will not hearken unto the priest ... shall die." There was reason, then, why no reproof should be given to the people,— they were past help. How clear is the reference to the Pentateuch in this passage! A very striking instance of quotation is found in chapter iv., 10. The prophet is describing the suffering that shall come upon the people for their sins; and he tells them, "They shall eat and not be satisfied" (c.v., "not have enough"). In Leviticus xxvi., 26, where the Lord threatens calamities if the people sin, he says, "When I have broken the staff of your bread, . . . ye shall eat and not be satisfied," — a verbal quotation. In the same verse is a distinct reference to Genesis xxviii., 14, and Leviticus xx., 20, 21: "They shall commit whoredom, and shall not increase." The original word for "increase," "to break forth," is used in the promise to Jacob, "And thou shalt spread abroad ["break forth"] to the west and to the east," etc. This use of the word is *peculiar* to the Pentateuch; and the threatening of not increasing is conformed to the passage referred to in Leviticus and many other places in the Law. In the thirteenth verse, the prophet accuses the people of sin, because they have done as wickedly as the nations which they were commanded to destroy: "They sacrifice upon the tops of the mountains, and burn incense upon the hills, under oaks and poplars and elms." In Deuteronomy xii., 2, where the practices of the nations are described, the same phrases are used, except that, in the last clause, the prophet has substituted specific names for "every green tree." In chapter v., 6, the prophet says it will not be with them now as it was of old, when they "go with their flocks and with their herds" to seek the Lord, for he will have withdrawn from them on account of their wickedness. In describing the sacrifices which the people offered to the Lord, in the Pentateuch the phrase "with your flocks and with your herds" is very common. Why were "the princes of Judah like them that remove the landmark" ("bound," c.v.), and upon whom the prophet declares that the Lord will "pour out his wrath like water"? Because in Deuteronomy xxvii., 17, it is said, "*Cursed* be he that removeth his neighbor's landmark." This reference is too striking to admit of doubt. And the prophet continues, "Ephraim is oppressed and crushed [c.v., broken in judgment] because he forsook the Lord"; just as it is declared it shall happen unto the nation, if they forsake God, in Deuteronomy xxviii., 33: "Thou shalt be only oppressed and crushed alway." In chapter v., 15, and vi., 1, we read, "In their affliction they will seek me early," and say, "Come, let us return unto the Lord, for he hath torn and he will heal us; he hath smitten and he will bind us up." This is a fulfilment of the prophecy in Deuteronomy iv., 30, "When thou art in affliction [c.v., tribulation], . . . in the latter days, and thou turn to the Lord thy God"; and in Deuteronomy xxxii., 39, "I kill and I make alive; I wound and I heal; neither is there any one that can deliver out of my hand." Compare with this Hosea v., 4, "I will tear, . . . and none shall deliver" (c.v., rescue). In chapter vii., 10, the people are reproved because, after all their afflictions, "they do not return to the Lord their God, nor seek him," as required in Deuteronomy iv., 29, 30. The declaration, "I will chastise them, as hath been proclaimed in their congregation" (c.v., "as their congregation hath heard"), chapter vii., 12, is to the point, as the laws were usually said to be proclaimed "to the congregation" in the Pentateuch. And here seems to be an explicit reference to punishments which had been threatened to the people at that time. In chapter viii., 6, there is an apparent reference in the original to the calf which was burned at

Horeb. The prophet says, "The calf of Samaria shall be broken in pieces" (made "kindlings" literally). In the twelfth verse there is the explicit declaration, "I have written to him the great things of my law"; or, as it should be translated, "I have *written* for him many laws; but they were counted as a strange thing." Here we have proof that the laws quoted were written, and these laws are found word for word in the Pentateuch. In the next verse is quoted the remarkable prophecy in Deuteronomy xxviii., 68, "They shall return to Egypt." In chapter ix., 4, in speaking of the calamity of the impending captivity, he says, "They shall not offer wine-offerings to the Lord; ... their sacrifices shall be unto them as the bread of mourners; all that eat thereof shall be polluted." In Leviticus xix. is a full statement of the defiled condition of all who are mourning. In the fifth verse, it is asked, "What will ye do in the solemn day [*i.e.*, feast days generally], and in the day of the feast of the Lord?" (*i.e.*, of the Passover, or some other of the three great feasts),— showing that feast days were observed at this time in Israel. The historical allusions in this chapter are too numerous for quotation. The feast of the tabernacles was celebrated in Israel; for in chapter xii., 9, we read, "I will yet make thee to dwell in tabernacles, as in the days of the solemn feasts" (feast). In verse 14, it is said of Ephraim, "He shall leave his blood upon him," which is a phrase used in the Law to show the penalty which hangs over the evil-doer, Leviticus xx., 9: "He that curseth his father or his mother, his blood shall be upon him," *i.e.*, he shall be put to death.

But I must not dwell upon the writings of this

prophet any longer. We find that he speaks of the Law, sometimes almost makes a formal quotation from it, and in almost innumerable instances makes use of its language. I have marked more than twice as many clear references to the Law as I have quoted. But, if these are not sufficient to convince the reader, no number would be. They most clearly identify the Law which was "written," and with which Hosea was familiar, with the Pentateuch of Ezra, of the son of Sirach, of Josephus, and of Martin Luther. His prophecy is as full of allusions to the Pentateuch, and his style partakes as much of its flavor, as the sermons of the Puritans do of the Bible; and one would as soon think of denying that John Robinson or John Cotton had our New Testament as that Hosea had our Pentateuch. It is admitted that the ritual and priesthood were existing in perfection, and that the Pentateuch was in the hands of Malachi substantially as we have it to-day, yet he does not refer to its contents or to the ceremonies of the ritual any more frequently than Hosea, who lived three hundred years before him. If Hosea makes as free use of it as Malachi, why is it not conclusive evidence that he had it? This inference can be overcome only by very weighty objections.

(9) I must make some examination of the writings of Amos, who was a little earlier than Hosea. In chapter ii., 7, our translation reads, "and turn aside the way of the meek": it should be rendered, "wrest the judgment of the weak," which agrees with Exodus xxiii., 6, "Thou shalt not wrest the judgment of thy poor." An abominable sin is spoken of in the same verse, which the Lord says "profanes his holy name,"

— a verbal reference to Leviticus xx., 3 : I will set my face against that man who " profanes my holy name." The wicked people are said (verse 8) "to lay themselves down upon clothes laid to pledge." Exodus xxii., 26, forbids this, and requires that "raiment taken to pledge" shall be delivered to the owner when "the sun goeth down." The phrase, verse 10, "and led you forty years in the wilderness," is a verbal quotation from Deuteronomy xxix., 5. The people are rebuked, verse 12, for giving "the Nazarites wine to drink." Why not? In Numbers vi., 3, the Nazarites' vow to abstain from wine is given.

The fourth chapter of Amos is so filled with references to the Pentateuch that a specific enumeration of them would be impossible in this study. Not less than a dozen instances of the use of language to be found in the different books of the Pentateuch could be quoted. I must content myself with a condensed summary, leaving the reader who is interested in this examination to pursue it into its details at his leisure. "Bring your sacrifices every morning," Numbers xxviii., 3, 4, "and your tithes after three years," Deuteronomy xiv., 28, which reads, "At the end of three years, thou shalt bring forth all the tithe of thine increase"; a very clear reference. "Offer a sacrifice of thanksgiving with leaven," Leviticus ii., 11, "and publish the free offerings," Leviticus xxii., 18. "I have given you want of bread," Leviticus xxvi., 26, "yet have ye not returned to me, saith the Lord." This last phrase is used several times in this chapter, and has evident reference to Deuteronomy iv., 30, where the people are exhorted, in their troubles, "to turn to the Lord their God." "I have smitten you with blasting and mildew," Deuteronomy xxviii., 22. "I have sent among you the pestilence, after the manner of Egypt," as predicted in Leviticus xxvi., 25; Deuteronomy vii., 15; xxviii., 27. In chapter v., 11, the prophet says, "Ye have built houses of hewn stone, but ye shall not dwell in them"; Deuteronomy xxviii., 30, where it is said, "Thou shalt build an house, and thou shalt not dwell therein." Further, the prophet says, "Ye have planted pleasant vineyards, but ye shall not drink wine of them"; predicted in Deuteronomy xxviii., 39, "Thou shalt plant vineyards, ... but shalt not drink of the wine." The prophet denounces them, because "they afflict the just, they take a bribe." Exodus xxiii., 8, Deuteronomy xvi., 19, declare "Thou shalt not wrest judgment, thou shalt not respect persons, neither take a gift" (bribe). In verse 17, he says, "I will pass through thee" as I passed through the land of Egypt on the dreadful night when the first-born were slain and you were preserved. Now you will be punished, and a great "wailing" will be heard among you, as a "great cry" was raised by Pharaoh and his servants. (Exodus xii., 30.) The Lord expresses his dislike (verses 21, 22) of their "feasts," their "solemn assemblies," their "burnt-offerings and meat-offerings," and of their "peace-offerings." (Numbers xxix., 25; Leviticus xxiii., 36; Deuteronomy xvi.) The prophet accuses the oppressors of the people of being so greedy of gain as to say, chap. viii., 5, "When will the *new moon* be gone that we may *sell corn*, and the Sabbath that we may *set forth* [open] wheat?" A remarkable resemblance exists in the original between the words marked in italics and those in Genesis xli.,

56, "And Joseph *opened* all the storehouses and *sold* unto the Egyptians." No "servile work" could be done on the new moon of the seventh month, or the beginning of the civil year. Leviticus xxiii., 24, 25. He further charges these greedy traffickers with "making the ephah small," Deuteronomy xxv., 14, "and the shekel great," Deuteronomy xxv., 13, "and falsifying the balances by deceit." Leviticus xix., 36, requires "just balances." When carried captive, the wicked people would not escape suffering, for the Lord says to them by the mouth of the prophet, chapter ix., 4, "Thence will I command the sword, and it shall slay them" (those in captivity), which is a reiteration of the threatening in Deuteronomy xxviii., 65, and Leviticus xxvi., 33, "I will draw out a sword after you among the heathen." In the same chapter, eighth verse, the Lord says, "I will destroy it [Israel] from off the face of the earth," which is a verbal repetition of the punishment threatened in Deuteronomy vi., 15, "The Lord thy God ... will destroy thee from off the face of the earth."

These quotations from Amos make it evident that he was familiar with the language of the Pentateuch. He rebukes Israel for violating the laws therein contained, and writes precisely as if the contents of that book were as familiar to him as the contents of the gospel were to John Bunyan. He calls the book by the name which it has had through all succeeding years up to his time. In giving a general reason for the punishment which would come upon the people, he says, in chapter ii., 4, "They have despised the Law of the Lord, and have not kept his commandments," a direct reference to the threat in Leviticus xxvi., 15, where it is said, "If ye shall despise my statutes," the most terrible calamities shall fall upon you. The customs, rites, worship which the prophet describes are all identical with those spoken of in "The Law."

It is important to remember that both Hosea and Amos prophesied in the kingdom of Israel. They addressed the rulers, princes, priests, and people of that nation as if *they* were familiar with the Law. They speak of them as keeping the feast days, the new moons, and the Sabbaths. Is it improbable that the people of Israel had a copy of the Law, whose contents are so fully stated in these prophecies? It is further to be remembered that Amos was "no prophet," that is, by education, "nor the son of a prophet"; he was a "shepherd and a gatherer of sycamore fruit." If, then, he was so familiar with "The Law," never having been educated in it, how much of its language must have been on the lips of those who had attended the schools of the prophets? There is more reason than some scholars are willing to allow for referring the Samaritan Pentateuch to a much earlier age than is commonly assigned to it. It is by no means improbable that copies of "The Law" existed in the northern kingdom before the captivity, and that the people who were left in the land had copies with them, and that it has been handed down among that people from age to age, to the present day. If such a supposition is reasonable, the existence of the Samaritan Pentateuch is evidence of the high antiquity of the Hebrew Pentateuch.

But I do not rest this argument on any such basis. I am tracing references to "The Law," the Pentateuch, back through the Hebrew writings that have come down to us; and we find abundant evidence of its existence in the writings of the two prophets who were sent to prophesy to the kingdom of Israel. But this aside. We must pursue our inquiry still further.

10. Next in order comes the prophecy of Joel, who was a little the predecessor of Amos, at least in the opinion of some scholars; but he prophesied to the kingdom of Judah.

The prophecy of Joel is very brief, covering but a few pages. The whole spirit of his prophecy is derived from "The Law." His promises and threatenings are all derived from those contained in "The Law." He says, "The meat-offering and the drink-offering is cut off from the house of the Lord; the priests mourn." "The harvest of the field is perished, the river is dried up, the fig-tree languisheth; ... call a solemn assembly," for the "locust hath eaten" up the harvest. Compare with these expressions Deuteronomy xxviii., 38-42. In the second chapter, the prophet directs them to call an assembly. "Blow ye the trumpet," says he. In Numbers x., 3, we find that this was the appointed method of calling an assembly. He says, describing the locusts, "There hath not been ever the like, neither shall there be any more after it, even to the years of many generations." This is a clear reference to Exodus x., 14, where, describing the locusts of the plague in Egypt, the writer says, "Before them there were no such locusts as they, neither after them shall there be such." In chapter ii., 13, the prophet exhorts the people to repent, assuring them that the Lord God "is gracious and merciful, slow to anger, and of great kindness"; an assurance which he could well give, for, Exodus xxxiv., 6, the Lord himself descended in a cloud, and proclaimed, "The Lord God, merciful and gracious, long-suffering, and abundant in goodness and truth." The prophet further says that the Lord will leave a blessing behind him, "a meat-offering and a drink-offering." Most earnestly he implores the people "to blow the trumpet, to proclaim a solemn assembly, to appoint a congregation, ... to let the priests weep between the porch and the altar, and say, Spare thy people, O Lord, and give not their heritage to reproach, that the heathen should use a by-word against them" (marginal reading). In Deuteronomy xxviii., 37, the people are threatened, if they sin, with the punishment of becoming "a proverb and a by-word among all nations." The reference is clear. Joel's prophecy is filled with Mosaic terms, and with the spirit and letter of the Law. Let it be remembered that Hosea, Amos, and Joel, whose references to Deuteronomy are so numerous, wrote a century and more before Hilkiah forged it, according to Kuenen.*

11. The testimony of two more books yet remains to be examined, the Proverbs and Psalms. In Ecclesiastes and Solomon's Song, we find nothing to our purpose, nor should we expect to. Nor should we expect to find much light on our theme in the Book of Proverbs. The subject of the book forbids it. Yet even here are there some hints of the existence of the Pentateuch.

* Yet, notwithstanding this evidence that the prophetic writings are saturated with the spirit and sprinkled all over with the phrases and ceremonies of the Pentateuch, a writer in the *Unitarian Review* for November, 1880, p. 427, asks in a tone of haughty challenge, "What reference to Mosaic law or Mosaic rites can you find in any of the earlier prophets?" "What appeal to their authority?"

King Lemuel's mother taught him, chapter xxxi., 5, that princes should not drink wine lest they "forget the Law, and pervert the judgment of any that are afflicted." Deuteronomy xxiv., 17, Exodus xxiii., 6, "Thou shalt not pervert judgment." In chapter xxviii., 4, 7, 9, "The Law" is spoken of. So also in chapter xxix., 18, we read, "He that keepeth the Law, happy is he," "but where there is no vision the people perish." Other passages of like character are found in the book which it is unnecessary to quote, as they add nothing to our argument. Davidson says, Vol. II., p. 342, "The Proverbs are ethical maxims *deduced from the Mosaic Law* and Divine Providence." The Book of Psalms contains lyric poems, for the most part, which were composed during a long period of the nation's existence. Some were probably composed before the time of David, many by him, and by his contemporaries and immediate successors, and some as late as after the return from captivity. If we could certainly select those of the earliest date, they would be much more to our purpose than those composed at a later period. As in many cases such a distinction cannot accurately be made, I shall quote from those which are more generally conceded to be of the earlier class, after I have drawn a few illustrations from those of a confessedly later period. The seventy-eighth psalm is supposed to have been written much later than the time of David. It is an historical poem, and repeats the most prominent incidents recorded in the Pentateuch. It speaks distinctly of the "covenant of God," and declares that the people refused in early times "to walk in his Law"; that "he established a testimony in Jacob, and appointed a Law in Israel," which he commanded the fathers to "make known to their children." Deuteronomy iv., 9, vi., 7, xi., 19, require that the Law should be taught to the children. The use of the language of the Pentateuch in this psalm is so pervading that I must ask readers to examine it for themselves in connection with this argument. To make quotations is impossible. Psalm cxix. is a very artistic poem, constructed with express reference to the Law, the statutes, the commandments, and the judgments of the Lord. Through one hundred and seventy-six verses, it labors, with all variety of phrase, to extol "The Law" of the Lord, and inculcate obedience to all its "statutes." In Psalm xcvii., the writer says that the Lord spake to his people "in the cloudy pillar; they kept his testimonies and the ordinance that he gave them." In Psalm lxxxix., 30–32, the writer, enumerating the calamities which shall rest upon the house of David, says, in the name of the Lord, "If his children forsake my Law, and walk not in my judgments; if they break my statutes, and keep not my commandments; then will I visit their transgression with the rod." Moses is spoken of as one to whom God had made himself known, ciii., 7; cv., 26; cvi., 16, 23, 32. These psalms are also filled with the incidents and language of the Pentateuch. In Psalm xix. there is a comparison made between the instruction given in the works of Nature and that which is given in "The Law of the Lord." "The Law of the Lord is perfect, converting the soul; the testimony of the Lord is sure, making wise the simple. The statutes of the Lord are right, rejoicing the heart; the commandment of the Lord is pure, enlightening the eyes. The fear [by metonymy, that which teaches us the fear] of the Lord is clean, enduring forever; the judgments of the Lord are true and righteous altogether." In Psalm xl., 8, we have a very clear statement of the existence of books in the time of David. "In the volume of the book it is written of me, . . . Thy law is within my heart." As it has been suggested that this may be a figurative reference to God's purposes, not to any literal volume, I do not press the inference that it refers to the *Book of the Law*, but simply say that it proves the existence of *written books* in the time of David; and we have seen already that, I. Kings ii., 3, David charges Solomon to keep the "statutes and commandments and judgments and testimonies" of the Lord, "as it is written in the Law of Moses." The poem and the history agree. In Psalm i., 2, it is said that the delight of the good man "is in the Law of the Lord, and in his Law doth he meditate day and night."

These references to the Pentateuch, under the same names which we have found in use from the time of Paul and the Son of Sirach, are proof of the existence of the same work which Paul and the Son of Sirach used, unless some proof can be brought that it was remodelled between these periods. Of such a transformation, history does not record a syllable: therefore the work is the same as that to which David and the Psalmists alluded, as that which Paul and the Son of Sirach used, unless internal evidence, derived from the book itself, can be brought to show the contrary. To that internal evidence, I shall attend in due time. I now confine myself to the historical evidence.

But we find not only the old names, but also the

style of the Pentateuch introduced into the Psalms, its facts alluded to, its rites mentioned. I will notice a few of the latter. In Psalm xix., 1, there is the same distinction between the heavens and the firmament as in Genesis i. The word "firmament" is a peculiar one, and is doubtless used by the Psalmist on that account. Psalm xxxiii., 6, 7, teaches us that "By the word of the Lord were the heavens made" (Genesis i., 14, "And God said, Let there be lights in the firmament"), "and all the host of them by the breath of his mouth" (Genesis ii., 1, "Thus the heavens and earth were finished, and all the host of them"). "He gathereth the waters of the sea together as a heap" (Genesis i., 9, "And God said, Let the waters ... be gathered together into one place"). In Psalm lxxxi., 3-5, there is a direct reference to the time when a statute there named was enacted: "Blow the trumpet in the new moon" (Numbers x., 10, "In the beginnings of your month [*i.e.*, new moons], ye shall blow with the trumpets"), "in the time appointed, on our solemn feast day; for this is a statute for Israel and a law of the God of Jacob. This he ordained ... when he went out through [of] the land of Egypt." Verse 6, "I removed from his shoulder the burden" (Exodus i., 11). In Psalm xv., 3-5, we read that a good man "backbiteth not with his tongue" (Leviticus xix., 16), "nor taketh up a reproach against his neighbor" (Exodus xxiii., 1). "He putteth not out his money to usury" (Exodus xxii., 25), "nor taketh a reward against the innocent" (Exodus xxiii., 8). "He sweareth to his own hurt, and changeth not" (Numbers xxx., 2). These references are all too distinct to be mistaken.

"Burnt-offerings and sin-offerings" are spoken of in xl., 6; li., 19; lxvi., 13, 15: "I will go into thy house with burnt-offerings; ... I will offer unto thee burnt sacrifices of fatlings, with the incense of rams." Psalm cxxxiii., the "precious ointment that ran down on Aaron's beard" refers to his anointing (Leviticus viii., 12), where Moses is said to pour the "anointing oil" on Aaron's head.

It is not necessary to accumulate these quotations any further. It is evident that, upon the supposition of the existence and familiar use of the Pentateuch by the writers of the Psalms, we could not expect to find more frequent allusions to the book, nor more evident use of its words and phrases, than we do find. Hence, the argument is as full and cogent from this quarter as is required for my purpose.

I have now closed my examination of the historical and poetical writings of the Jewish nation back to the time of David. And, all through both classes of writings, we find not only the *title* of the Pentateuch named in references to it, but we also find constant use of its *style*, and allusion to its rites, ceremonies, and laws. I hesitate not to say that no writing which has come down to our day from a remote antiquity can show such an array of historical evidence attesting its age as the writings of the Jews furnish to the existence of the Pentateuch in the time of David. The book which David referred Solomon to as the "Law of Moses," in which were "written the statutes, commandments, judgments, and testimonies of the Lord," is the book which now lies open before me, or else I have no reason or right to speak of the history of Thucydides as being in our hands. Those who are not accustomed to inquiries of this kind may not be aware of the superior amount and quality of the evidence which can be adduced in favor of the existence of the Pentateuch in the time of David, over that which can be produced in favor of the early origin of any other work of remote antiquity which has come into our hands, and which, nevertheless, we accept as being sustained by all the evidence which, under the circumstances, could be expected.

Let us remember, too, the period at which we have arrived. We are within four hundred years or less of the time in which Moses lived, who is supposed by David to have written these laws. The golden age of Hebrew literature is fixed at this period. A glorious temple was to be erected in which the worship of Jehovah, as prescribed in "The Law," could be offered. The schools of the prophets had been sending out scholars into all parts of the land for a hundred years. It is incredible that a book containing the fundamental laws of such a nation, on an obedience to which rested their national destiny, could have been so universally referred to their great law-giver, if indeed he had no hand in its composition. Had we no fragments of history relating to the period between David and Moses, we could not hesitate to refer the book to him to whom it was referred at this period. The men of that age were abundantly capable of determining such a question. They were under the most imperative obligation to determine it correctly, and there is no more reason, historically, to suppose them to be mistaken than we have to suppose that the English monarchs and scholars are mistaken in referring the Doomsday Book to the time of William the Conqueror.

SECTION IV. FROM DAVID TO MOSES.

As far as external historical evidence is concerned, I might pause here. But there are some earlier writings, some portions of which were composed probably before the time of David, or during his reign,— namely, Joshua and Judges; and some which, though relating to the times previous to him, were not composed till a later period,— namely, the Books of Joshua and Samuel.

To understand the value of the evidence rendered by these books to the antiquity of the Pentateuch, a word is necessary respecting their age and contents. The Book of Joshua was written before the close of the reign of Solomon, if we can rely upon the statement made in chapter xvi., 10, where it is said, "The Canaanites dwell among the Ephraimites [in Gezer] unto this day." But, in I. Kings ix., 16, we read that Pharaoh "took Gezer, burned it with fire, slew the Canaanites, and gave it as a present to his daughter, Solomon's wife." The book may have been composed earlier, even in the reign of Saul, or during the life of Samuel. There is nothing in the style or contents of the book which requires a later author. The contents of the book are such as rather to forbid than admit any specific quotations from the Pentateuch, consisting, as they do in the first half, of a description of passing over Jordan, and of the battles of the conquest, and, in the last half, of a condensed statement of the boundaries of the tribes and their cities.*

The Book of Judges tells us, in chapter i., 21, that "the Jebusites dwell with the children of Benjamin in Jerusalem unto this day," which shows, if the passage can be relied upon, that the book, or the main part of it, must have been written before the end of David's reign, since in II. Samuel, chapter v., 6-8, we learn that David drove the Jebusites out of Jerusalem, and took the stronghold of Zion and dwelt in it. A passage in the appendix of the book, which was added at a later date, chapter xviii., 30, would probably place this addition as late as 721 B.C. "The day of the captivity of the land" is spoken of. There is nothing in the language or contents of the body of the book to forbid its composition in the early years of the monarchy, since its descriptions of the anarchical condition of the people have very much the appearance of an apology or good reason for a stronger and consolidated government, as well as of an illustration of the peril of "doing evil in the sight of the Lord." The subject of both the book and its appendix is such as not to require or even permit many references to the Pentateuch, made up as it is of battles and exploits of heroes and heroines, and devoting four chapters to the freaks and

* Davidson says (*Intro. O. T.*, Vol. I., p. 415): "The ecclesiastical state of the people under Joshua appears to have been in accordance with the divine law. There was the ark of the covenant, priests, a high priest Eleazer, Levitical cities. Circumcision and the passover were observed. The tabernacle was set up, and the congregation assembled beside it. [Dr. Oort, *Bible for Learners*, says, "The tabernacle never really existed except in the imagination of the writer" (of Exodus), who lived after the captivity.] The Reubenites, Gadites, and half-tribe of Manasseh 'kept all that Moses, the servant of God, commanded them.'"

follies and feats and gallantries of the renowned athlete, Samson.

The Books of Samuel, down to the reign of David, appear to be closely connected with the succeeding history, and very probably were the production of the author of the history of that reign, whose writings were used by the author of the Book of Kings, who wrote at the commencement of the captivity, 586 B.C. During this tumultuous period of establishing the monarchy, but little reference would be made, in brief annals, to rituals and customs. Weightier and novel matters would press upon the writer's attention. And in all these writings we cannot rely upon any stronger evidence of the age of the Pentateuch than is furnished by the opinion of the age in which they were written, as expressed by their authors. It is true that they did not rely wholly upon tradition. They had, apparently, in their hands scraps of records and songs which furnished some written testimony to the customs and laws of this period, and to the existence of the Mosaic ritual. These obscure references and passing hints we shall do well to notice and weigh.

In I. Samuel i., 3, we read that Hannah and her husband, a hundred years before the time of David, "went up yearly to worship and to sacrifice unto the Lord of hosts, in Shiloh," where the tabernacle was. In chapter i., 21, 22, the writer tells us that the journey was repeated the next year by the father alone, and that the second year the child Samuel was with them. This "yearly" journey was required by "The Law" at the feast of the passover, but we do not read of it again in the book, showing how many things customary are not named. We read of the offering of "burnt-offerings" and "peace-offerings" at different times and at different places, since no spot had been selected as the permanent resting-place of the ark. There are, also, found some phrases in the Books of Samuel which the historian evidently took from the Books of Moses ; but as he wrote at as late a period as is covered by some of the books already examined, and as his style would only prove the existence of the Pentateuch when he wrote, I will not occupy much space by making quotations. In I. Samuel, chapter xii., 14, Samuel says to the people, "If ye will not rebel against the commandment of the Lord," it will be well with you ; "but if ye rebel against the commandment of the Lord, then shall the hand of the Lord be against you, as it was against your fathers." This is obviously said in reference to the Law, for "the commandment," "the testimony," are often used for the Pentateuch. The writer of the Book of Judges, chapter iii., 4, says, "They [the nations not conquered] were to prove Israel, . . . to know whether they would hearken unto the commandments of the Lord, which he had *commanded their fathers* by the *hand of Moses.*" In Joshua i., 7, 8, the Lord is represented as thus addressing Joshua : " Be thou strong and very courageous, that thou mayest observe to do according to all the *Law which Moses*, my servant, commanded thee. . . . This *Book of the Law* shall not depart out of thy mouth, . . . that thou mayest do all that is written therein." In chapter viii., 30, 31, we read that "Joshua built an altar, . . . as Moses the servant of the Lord commanded the children of Israel, as it *is written in the Book of the Law of Moses.*" In chapter xxiii , 6, we read of what "is written in the Book of the Law of Moses"; and in chapter xxiv., 26, we read that "Joshua wrote these words in the Book of the Law of God."

Such are the names given in these early annals to the book or code by which the people were governed. Let us now see if the references to it or the customs of the period render it certain that our Pentateuch is intended by these names. The priests are represented in Joshua as "bearing the ark," and the "ark of the covenant," and the "ark of the Lord," and "the ark of the testimony"; and "Phinehas, the son of Aaron," is said to have "stood before the ark of the covenant of God in those days," in the Book of Judges ; and in I. Samuel it is spoken of ten times, and in II. Samuel five times. In Joshua xviii., 1, "the tabernacle of the congregation" is said to "be set up at Shiloh," and it is mentioned again xxii., 19 ; and three times it is spoken of in Samuel. The "curtains" of the dwelling-place of the ark are mentioned in II. Samuel vii., 2, and in the sixth verse the "tent and tabernacle" are spoken of, describing the original tabernacle accurately, the "tent" signifying the outward covering of skins and cloth of goat's hair, and "the tabernacle" signifying the "curtains of fine twined linen and blue and purple and scarlet," Exodus xxvi., 1, 14. This passage shows how carefully the material and form of the ancient tabernacle had been preserved through all ages and vicissitudes, amid repairs and renewals down to the time of David, a period of about four hundred years, when we find him ambitious to erect a more imposing structure for the administration of the ritual. We read, in

I. Samuel xxi., 6, of the "shew bread" which was in the tabernacle at Nob, chapter xxii., 11, and which was "hallowed bread," of which David and his men were permitted to eat after much deliberation, as it was sacredly set apart for the priests, Leviticus xxiv., 9. In I. Samuel, during times bordering upon those of the Judges, we read frequently of "offerings" and "sacrifices," offered apparently at places where the "tabernacle" was from time to time located, and sometimes on altars built for the occasion.

These records of religious observances are quite frequent, though brief; but they are hints of what existed and was common, as the "yearly sacrifice" to which the people are said to go up is mentioned specially but three times. And it is to be remembered that these were turbulent times, and the writer of Judges does not dwell upon the years of peace, but describes almost exclusively the insurrections and forays and personal exploits of the time. We read of "priests" in Joshua and Judges and Samuel, and of their presence at the place of the tabernacle. There is no evidence which is decisive that any service which was allotted by the Law to a priest was performed by any other person. In the case of Samuel, there are two or three instances in which he may have offered sacrifice; but it is by no means clear that even in those a priest was not in attendance, though not spoken of. But, granting that Samuel did offer sacrifices two or three times, it does not follow that it was lawful, but rather that he violated the Law. And, further, if we can rely upon the record, the relation of Samuel to the priesthood was unique; and he may have felt authorized to act as a priest in certain contingencies, if he did so. In either view of his action, it does not furnish even a presumption against the existence of the ritual; much less does it furnish an argument against its existence.

Did I not fear that I should utterly exhaust the patience of my readers, I should like to refer to some yet more obscure indications of the existence of the Pentateuch contained in these fragmentary sketches of the earliest anarchical times, and yet so exact as to command attention. I must satisfy my desire to give a specimen of them: I. Samuel i., 11, "And there shall no razor come upon his head"; a literal statement of the Law of the Nazarite, Numbers vi., 5. Chapter i., 24, she "took three bullocks and an ephah of flour" for her offering; just the right proportion of flour prescribed to a bullock, Numbers xxviii., 12. Chapter ii., 2, "Neither is there any rock like our God," is literally taken from Deuteronomy xxxii., 30. The departure from the ritual by the wicked sons of Eli is described in chapter ii., 13–15, in not "burning the fat" and the "sodden meat" which were prescribed in Leviticus vi., 28, and vii., 31–35. In verses 18, 19, the child Samuel's "linen ephod" is mentioned, and his "little coat" (robe), which was the priest's garment worn under the "ephod," both described in Exodus xxviii., 6, 31. In chapter iii., 3, we read of the "lamp which burnt" in the place "where the ark of God was," Exodus xxvii., 21. In chapter iii., 14, we read of the "sacrifice" (*zabach*) and "offering" (*mincah*) required by the Law in many places. I have already alluded to the frequency with which the "ark of the covenant" is mentioned. Chapter vi., 6, speaks of the "hardening" of the people's hearts as the heart of "Pharaoh was hardened," Exodus xii., 31. In chapter vii., 9, we read that "Samuel took a sucking lamb, and offered it for a burnt-offering wholly to the Lord," Leviticus xxii., 7. Chapter viii., 3, Samuel's "sons took bribes and perverted judgment," Exodus xxiii., 8. Chapter ix., 24, "And the cook took up [heaved up] the shoulder, and set it before Saul," Exodus xxix., 27. Chapter x., 25, "Samuel wrote in a book the manner of the kingdom," Deuteronomy xvii., 18, 19. Chapter xx., 5, 6, "To-morrow is the new moon," said David, "let me go . . . to Bethlehem, for there is a yearly sacrifice there for all the family," Numbers x., 10; xxviii., 11. Verse 26, "Saul . . . thought something had befallen him [David], he is not clean; surely he is not clean," Leviticus vii., 20, 21. Chapter xxviii., 3, "And Saul put away those that had familiar spirits and wizards out of the land," Deuteronomy xviii., 11, 12. Chapter xxx., 7, 8, "And David said to Abiathar, the priest, bring me hither the ephod [in which were the Urim and Thummim]. . . . And David inquired of the Lord," Numbers xxvii., 21. Frequently the "Lord" is said to be "inquired of" in the life of David. In II. Samuel vi., 2–17, we read of the "ark of the Lord and the cherubim," and of the death of Uzzah for touching it, Numbers iv., 15.

In Judges i., 20, we read that "they gave Hebron unto Caleb, as Moses said," Numbers xiv., 24; Joshua xiv., 9, 13. In chapter ii., 17, 20, 22, the people are charged with going "a whoring after other gods, and turning quickly out of the way which their fathers walked in, . . . transgressing my covenant, which their fathers did keep" (chap. iii., 6); and the children of

Israel "took their [Canaanites'] daughters to be their wives, and gave their daughters to their sons, and served their gods," and, verse 4, did not "hearken unto the commandments of the Lord, which he commanded the fathers by the hand of Moses." Read the Law, Exodus xxxiv., 15, 16. The "ephod," in which were the Urim and Thummim, is spoken of as if essential even in forbidden forms of consultation, viii., 27; xvii., 5; xviii., 14, 17, 18. In xiii., 19, we read that "Manoah took a kid with a meat [meal] offering, and offered it upon a rock to the Lord." This kind of offering is required, Numbers xv., 24. "Burnt-offerings" and "peace-offerings" are mentioned in xiii., 16; xx., 26; xxi., 4. "The ark of the covenant" is spoken of, xx., 27. "The house of God in Shiloh," that is the "tabernacle," is spoken of in xviii., 31, and very probably also in xix., 18; xx., 18, 26, 31; and xxi., 2. Phinehas, the grandson of Aaron, "stands before the ark," xx., 28. "A man plucked off his shoe, and gave it to his neighbor to confirm" a bargain respecting marriage under peculiar circumstance, as reported in Ruth iv., 8. The Law is found in Deuteronomy xxv., 9. A reference is also made in iv., 12, to Genesis xxxviii., 29.

But I must refrain, or patience will be utterly exhausted. I wished to quote some of my notes on Joshua, especially those including passages where it is said that something was done "as Moses the servant of the Lord commanded," as, in chapter xi., 12, "Joshua smote all the cities of those kings and all the kings of them with the edge of the sword, and he utterly destroyed them, as Moses the servant of the Lord commanded." The command of Moses is in

Numbers xxxiii., 52, and Deuteronomy vii., 2, "Thou shalt smite them and utterly destroy them; thou shalt make no covenant with them, nor shew mercy unto them." I leave them all, and close here the direct historical or external evidence of the antiquity of the Pentateuch. Fragmentary and obscure as many of these notices and references are in these early books, I submit that they are as numerous and as explicit as any reasonable critic would expect to find. I confess to my own surprise at finding so many. Only Hebraists can estimate the loss I feel in not being able to make these quotations from the original language, that their force might be fully estimated.*

I cannot better meet the objection which is raised against the existence of the Mosaic ritual during the time of the Judges and Samuel, founded upon the infrequent mention of it and of its observance, than by refer-

---

* Much has been made by Kuenen, Graf, Prof. Smith, and others, of the use of the words, "the priests, the Levites," in Deuteronomy xvii., 9, 18, and elsewhere, without the copulative conjunction, "and," as if it proved that there was no distinct portion of the tribe of Levite priests before the captivity. But the same formula is used *after* the captivity (Nehemiah x, 29, 35; xi., 20; I. Chronicles ix., 2; II. Chronicles v., 5; xxiii., 18; xxx., 27; Isaiah lxvi., 21; Jeremiah xxxiii., 18), showing that, however it is to be explained, it certainly does not mean that all Levites were priests or could be; but undoubtedly it meant that all priests were Levites of the tribe of Levi, as the history testifies. There are only twenty-four places in the Old Testament where this phrase is used, and these may well be explained by the not unusual grammatical *asyndetic construction*, where "conjunctions which serve to connect words and phrases are omitted," as in Genesis xxxi., "yesterday [and] the day before"; Judges xix., 2, "a year [and] four months"; Habakkuk iii., 11, "sun [and] moon"; Nahum iii., 1, "it is full of lies [and] robbery"; Isaiah lxiii., 11, "Moses [and] his people"; Proverbs xxii., 21, "words [and] truth"; Zechariah i., 13, "words [and] consolations"; Exodus xxiv., 5, "offerings [and] peace-offerings." These examples must suffice. To build up a theory of the Jewish priesthood on this phrase used but twenty-four times in opposition to the clear and explicit declarations of both the law in the Pentateuch and the testimony of subsequent history is erecting a pyramid on its apex.

ring to the early history of the colony of Plymouth. That the Pilgrims had the Bible and ministers and churches and regular services on Sunday, everybody knows. William Bradford, for many years governor of the colony, wrote a history of it down to 1646, or for twenty-six years after the colony landed at Plymouth. It makes an octavo volume of four hundred and forty-four pages. I have looked through its pages to see how he treats the subject of religion,— its ministry, its church, its ordinances, its Bible. I may have overlooked some instances in which he speaks of them, but I am confident they can be but few. He mentions "the Lord's day" but twice; he speaks of "ministers" but fifteen times; of the "church" but twenty times; of "baptism" but once; and in every instance very briefly. Four times he speaks of the "Scriptures"; four times of "the word of God"; and once of "the infallible word of God,"— evidently meaning in all these cases the Bible. There are repeated quotations from the Bible, and its language is used frequently; and sometimes the book and the chapter and verse are mentioned from which the quotation is taken. And the "gospel" is spoken of ten times as if the New Testament was meant in distinction from the Old; and once "the pure Testament of Christ" is named, with evident reference to the New Testament. There is one reference to "neglecting hearing the word on the Lord's day." The choice of a "pastor" is spoken of three or four times. Two instances of setting apart a "day of humiliation" are recorded. "Taxing for preaching" is once spoken of. And yet this history is written in a religious spirit, and "God's providence" is mentioned on almost every page. Now, the very brief Book of Judges covers a period ten times as long as Bradford's history does, and would give room for ten times less reference to the ritual than Bradford makes to the Pilgrims' ecclesiastical affairs, were the book as large as Bradford's; but, if its size is taken into the account also, there would be eighty times less chance in Judges to treat of religious rites and books than in Bradford; and if Bradford does not speak of the Bible in any phraseology, under any name, but about sixteen times, how many times could we expect Judges to speak of the "Law of Moses," on the supposition that it was used as freely and observed as scrupulously during that period as the Bible was by the Pilgrims? An answer to this question gives the weight of the objection named above, and it is found to be of no value. And, in farther confirmation of this estimate of the little weight to be attached to this objection, another cause of the infrequent reference to the Law and its ritual is found in Dr. Kuenen's *Religion of Israel*. He says (Vol. II., p. 293), "A temporary abeyance of the ritual legislation is not inconceivable" under "kings indisposed" to regard it. Much more, then, may we suppose that its observance was frequently held in "abeyance" during the stormy times of the Judges, and the convulsions which attended the establishment of the monarchy.

If "amidst arms laws are silent," we should not expect to hear anything of ritual observances during the tumults of the Judges.

This would be the place to examine the evidence which the Book of Deuteronomy furnishes of the existence of the Book of the Law, the ritual code, were it not that the references to it are so intimately connected with the internal evidence, the second division of my Study, as to make its examination at that time most convenient and suitable. It must suffice, therefore, to say here and now that the existence of some such book or code is clearly implied, if not necessitated, by the laws quoted and amended, and the ceremonies modified and the demands withdrawn. These will be fully examined and illustrated in due time, and are of such a nature and so numerous as to bind all the previous historical evidence back to a date as early as the death of Moses.

We have now traced back through a period of over a thousand years notices of a work containing the laws which governed the Jews. We find that the various *names* by which it is called, beginning with the New Testament, in all the works which have come down to our time, are repeated in an unbroken series back to the time of Joshua. "The Law," "The Law of Moses," "The Law of the Lord," "The Book of the Law," "The Book of the Law by the hand of Moses," "The Book of the Law of the Lord," "The statutes and commandments of the Lord," are used as names to designate the Pentateuch from the days of Paul to the days of Joshua. And, further than this, we have found that the *passages which are quoted* by all this series of writers from the book referred to under those names are contained in the Pentateuch, and are often quoted with verbal exactness, even when the language of the Pentateuch is peculiar. And, still further, we have found that *peculiar words and phrases* are used frequently in all these writings, which are most obviously taken from "The Law," showing that it was a book whose contents were as familiar to these writers as the language of the New Testament is to the preachers of our day. In a word, we have found all the evidence that could be expected, and vastly more than is found for the antiquity of any other writing of an age even much less remote.

The whole atmosphere of these books is fragrant with the incense which rose from the Law, and the whole elaborate, magnificent ritual of the nation is found imbedded in it. Our Pentateuch did exist in their day. It must have existed, or all historical evidence is false and worthless.

It is hardly necessary to allude to an objection to the early origin of the Pentateuch which was raised by a former class of critics, and pressed with great vehemence. It was maintained that the art of writing, even if known, was not sufficiently advanced to produce such works as the Pentateuch as early as the time of Moses. Modern discoveries, however, in Egypt and Chaldea and Babylonia have removed all doubt that writing was common in all these countries as early as the age of Moses. The walls of the tombs and temples of Egypt are adorned with representations of scribes engaged in writing; and a room has been opened in one of the great palaces which is called a "library," showing that works were collected for use. Cloth, papyrus, skins, and stones were used for engraving and writing. Rituals and financial documents of almost every kind are found among the relics in the tombs. In Chaldea and Babylonia, also, writings are found on tablets of hardened clay, showing that poems were written in the Ur of Abraham before he was born. The Legends of Izdubar are about half as long as the Iliad, and they were written five centuries before the birth of Moses. And from that remote date, 2000 B.C., down, we have writings of every kind,— accounts, deeds, biographies, histories, legends, etc.,— demonstrating not only the possibility, but the probability that the great law-giver of Israel would commit his ritual and code to writing, as it is affirmed in the Pentateuch that he did. But I have lingered on this effete objection longer than its inherent weight justifies; yet as an illustration of the baselessness of many other objections, and of the confirmation of the antiquity of the Pentateuch found in the abundance of books and writings of various kinds of a far earlier date even, it seemed necessary to say as much as this respecting it.

It may be expected that something will be said at this point respecting the marvellous events which are recorded in the historical portions of the Pentateuch. As this Study is not exegetical, but historical, such an inquiry does not fall within my subject; at least, I have no occasion to treat of these marvellous events any further than their record affects the question of the age and origin of the Pentateuch. The historical book of Genesis closes at least two centuries before the time of the Hebrew law-giver, and is evidently composed of such traditions, recorded and oral, as had come down to his time. We have no conclusive proof that the wonderful things there recorded are true, or that they ever transpired; and the contents of the book do not in the slightest degree weigh against the opinion that it was written or compiled in the Mosaic age. Respecting the history in Exodus up to the arrival at Sinai, it is probable, all the circumstances taken into consideration, that it was not written till many years after the events described took place, and may not have been written till many years after the death of Moses, though it must have been written while the "archaic language" was in use.* The nature and extent of the wonders in Egypt may have been exaggerated, as repeated from father to son; and it is not impossible that a literally correct account is not given of the evils which befell the Egyptians at that time, and the exact circumstances of their deliverance. Very probable it is so. No blame can attach to the writer, whoever he was, who gathered up these oral reports of the causes which led to the escape of his nation from bondage, and what befell the people in their flight. An interval

* It is hardly necessary to remind the intelligent reader that passages have occasionally found their way into the text which were at first only marginal notes and explanations of names and places,— which has happened to all ancient writings, and by no means proves the composition of the work itself to have been at as late a period as that of the note. A few specimens of these later notes will be given. Genesis xii., 6, "And the Canaanite was then in the land." Genesis xiii., 7, "And the Canaanite and the Perizzite dwelt in the land." These sentences were added after the conquest. Genesis xxiii., 2, "In Kirjath-arba; the same is Hebron." The last words were written after the conquest, to define an ancient city. Another passage shows that the interpolated note was not written till after the monarchy was established: Genesis xxxvi., 31, "before there reigned any king over the land of Israel." The passage respecting the cessation of the manna (Exodus xvi., 35) belongs to the same class. Leviticus xviii., 28, "as it spued out the nations before you," is evidently a note. Deuteronomy ii., 12, contains another. So also Exodus vi., 20, and xi., 3, unless, as is more probable, the whole account, Exodus i.-xix., 25, was written later. "The meekness of the man Moses," Numbers xii., 3, is clearly a marginal note. These are specimens of the explanatory notes which have found their way into the text. Their parenthetical character most clearly shows that such was their origin, and they raise hardly the slightest antecedent presumption against the antiquity of the original work.

of forty or fifty years, perhaps more, after the death of Moses, a full century or more after they transpired, would be sufficient to magnify, in their narration, events which, in any point of view, must have been startling and destructive. Precisely what those calamities were, I have no occasion to inquire. That they were uncommon and very serious, is evident. It matters not, as far as this argument is concerned, whether they were miraculous or natural in the usual acceptance of these words.

The same remarks may be made respecting the description of the giving of the commandments at Sinai. They may have been, they were, written at the time; but the historian may not have known the precise circumstances under which they were given when he wrote the attached history, and intervening years and the descriptions of others may have magnified the wonderful phenomena of mountain scenery as it had appeared to persons born and reared in the level and fertile valley of the Nile. I enter into no speculation on this subject, but only say that such an origin will account fully for the coloring which is given them. Were these wonderful events accurately recorded, and were they stupendous miracles, the antiquity of the Pentateuch would not be in the least affected by it, for that is proved in an entirely independent manner. Almighty Power is amply equal to doing what is here recorded; and, if any one chooses that interpretation of these remarkable events, the way is open without in the slightest degree shaking the conclusion, otherwise reached, of the age and origin of the Pentateuch.

One word more, though not closely connected with

the subject. The Pentateuch, as well as the rest of the Bible, is written from a *religious point of view*, and everything which takes place is attributed to the direct act of God. So, when a person speaks what he or others think is the will of God, it is said that God speaks, that God commands, that God forbids. The same language is now used not only by ignorant, but by intelligent, religious people. Further than this, Seiler says, in his Hermeneutics, the Bible "sometimes describes events by representing as spoken things which had only happened, without the express words having been actually employed,"— as the thunder is said to be the voice of God, as God spake to Moses in the burning bush, whatever it may have been,— that is, taught him by it as a sign. So, probably, the supposed teaching of remarkable events is embodied by the historian in words which are attributed to God. But it is time to return to the direct discussion of my subject, which is not related except very remotely to any of these questions, any more than the age and authorship of *Gulliver's Travels* and *Robinson Crusoe* are related to, or depend upon, the authenticity, the truth of, the accounts recorded in them. The contents may be incredible, but their age and authorship may be indubitable. Things differing so widely must not be confounded with each other.*

* Great stress is laid upon the fact by many writers, and by Prof. Smith in particular, that "anointed stones" (*Matstsebahs*) were erected, and "carved images" set up by kings and priests until the captivity, and thus proving that the law against idol-worship was not in existence. But it is evident that many of these "anointed stones" and "carved images" were not made for worship, and were forbidden by the law only when worshipped. Not only were the curtains of the tabernacle "wrought with cherubim of cunning work" (Exodus xxxvi., 8), but two cherubim were made of pure gold to stand on either end of the mercy-

SECTION V. CONCLUSION OF THE HISTORICAL EVIDENCE.

Here I rest the *historical evidence* for the antiquity of the Pentateuch. Were there no internal evidence in support of the external, we should be obliged, by the laws of historical criticism, to accept "The Book of the Law of Moses" as originating in his age. That the last four books, or portions of them, indirectly profess to have been written in that age, is not disputed. The validity of this profession is sustained by the internal as well as by the external evidence, as I shall show. But, before examining it, I will quote some of the opinions of leading liberal, not to say radical, critics on the antiquity of portions, at least, and large ones, of the books contained in the Pentateuch, that the reader may see the extravagance of some recently broached hypotheses, and how very near these

seat in the Most Holy place, on the Most Holy ark (xxxvii., 10). The second commandment did not forbid making "carved images," but it forbid making carved work or any images *for worship* (Exodus xx., 4, 5). When Solomon erected his Temple, he not only covered the walls with "carvings of cherubim and palm-trees and open flowers," but he set up two pillars at the entrance of the Temple, covered all over with carvings of vines and pomegranates, and made a molten sea "which stood upon twelve oxen," and "between the ledges were lions, oxen, and cherubim," showing that Solomon did not interpret the law as forbidding making images for *ornament*, but for *gods* (I. Kings vi.). If any one should say that all this use of carved ornaments, and images of beasts and fruits and vines, shows either the absence of the law or its disregard, let him turn to Ezekiel, and he will find that his ideal temple is adorned in the same manner, as far as he gives a particular description of it. Not only were cherubim and palm-trees carved upon the walls of the temple, but each "cherub had two faces, the face of a man and the face of a young lion" (Ezekiel xli.). So the great reformer and composer of the law, as some maintain, did not hesitate to use "carved images" to ornament his ideal temple, while in his law — for it is maintained by these authors that Ezekiel wrote Leviticus xxvi. — he had *absolutely forbidden* all images for any use. So evident is it that the second commandment only forbade the use of images as representing Jehovah, and set up for worship.

able scholars come to sustaining the result of my own historical inquiry.

De Wette says (§ 162, b.), "He [Amos] must have had the Book of Genesis, *in its present form*, about 790 B.C." "Hosea (785 B.C.) affords us a trace of its existence. He must have known *the Book of Numbers*, as well as the original documents and later fragments of Genesis." "Isaiah (759 B.C.) evidently refers to Genesis." And "Micah (725 B.C.) refers to Numbers and Genesis." "The discovery of the Book of the Law in the Temple, under Josiah's reign, about 624 B.C., related in II. Kings xxii., is the first certain trace of the existence of the Pentateuch *in its present form*" (§162, a.). And he says (§ 12, b.), "Our present four books of Moses originated in the time of Solomon," 1000 B.C. De Wette decides that "the Elohim document was written in the time of Samuel or Saul" (1100 B.C.) (§ 158), and the "Jehovistic document before the reformation under Hezekiah took place," 726 B.C. (§ 159). But this whole hypothesis of the use of Elohistic and Jehovistic documents, especially after the Book of Genesis, is shown to be without sufficient reason, and all

---

I have carefully examined all the cases of disregard of the Levitical law referred to by Prof. Smith, which are recorded as taking place down to the time of David and a little after, and find not one which is not impliedly in violation of the law or excused on the ground of the unsettled state of the nation, or growing out of a false interpretation of the law itself. The worship of strange gods in the time of Solomon, and under his patronage, was not more antagonistic to the Levitical law than was the worship of images under the patronage of the Pope in the tenth century. The universal prevalence of taking oaths all over Christendom, and the numerous grounds of divorce in all Christian lands, would be greater evidence of the non-existence of the gospel history than the offering of sacrifices by Samuel and Saul and Solomon is of the non-existence of the Levitical law which permitted the priests alone to offer them,—if indeed these men and others did offer them, for often what one does by another as his agent one is said to do himself, as Solomon is said to have built the Temple, though he hewed neither stone nor timber.

conclusions drawn from it are therefore unreliable. The "archaic" words and phrases which Ewald and Gesenius and De Wette maintain are found in the Pentateuch are as numerous in what are called the "Jehovistic" documents as in the Elohistic; but the former, according to De Wette, was written about three hundred years after the latter. He says, "The Pentateuch was *completed* about the time of Josiah" (§ 12, b.).

Dr. Davidson (Vol. I., p. 133) says, "The present Pentateuch had been completed shortly before the reign of Josiah" (641 B.C.), "in the reign of Manasseh" (690 B.C.?) (p. 123). "The Book of the Law of Moses, spoken of II. Kings xiv., 6, may or may not have been the whole Pentateuch. The notice in question proceeds from the compiler of the Kings, who wrote after the present Pentateuch was completed.... In this passage, we understand *the Book of the Law to be coextensive with the Pentateuch*" (p. 119). "The same meaning may be assigned to the same phrase in II. Kings xxii., 8, 11, and II. Chronicles xxxiv., 14, 15," where Shaphan is said to have found "The Book of the Law in the house of the Lord." And Dr. Davidson goes so far as to say that it must have the same sense in II. Chronicles xvii., 9, where it is said Jehoshaphat (912 B.C.) sent out men to teach "the Book of the Law of the Lord through all the cities of Judah." This statement is made on the authority, as the writer of Chronicles says, of what he found "written in the Book of Jehu, the son of Hanani," whose works were a part of "the book of the kings of Israel." On this admission it is not easy to see why Dr. Davidson does not also admit that the Pentateuch, at least, may have been in existence at this time "in its present form." He does say with emphasis that "it is impossible to assign it to so late a date" as the time of Ezra (p. 122). He also maintains that Moses wrote not only the commandments, Exodus xx., but also xxi.–xxiii., 19; xxv.–xxxi. He further claims that Moses was the writer of Leviticus i.–vii., xi.–xvii., "which have the genuine Mosaic stamp" very perceptibly. Numbers i. "exhibits a minuteness, circumstantiality, and historical verisimilitude which scarcely allow of a different writer. *All is natural on the supposition of their belonging to the time of Moses.* Chapter iv. belongs to the same times; x., 1–8, must be regarded as Mosaic; xix. is a wilderness enactment. These are not the only parts of the three middle books of the Pentateuch written by Moses. The tabernacle was made in the wilderness, and the Levitical legislation was *Mosaic* in its origin and essence" (Vol. I., pp. 109–113). Here are about *thirty chapters* attributed to the pen of Moses in Exodus —Numbers by as radical a critic as Dr. Davidson. Lengerke places the Elohistic document in the time of Solomon and the Jehovistic in the time of Hezekiah. Tuch places the Elohistic document in the time of Saul, and the Jehovistic in the time of Solomon. Stähelin places the Elohistic document in the time of the Judges and the Jehovistic in the time of Manasseh. Ewald, whose theory of documents was peculiar and accepted by few or none, believed they were all written before the end of the seventh century B.C., and assumed nearly their present form (*History of Israel*, Vol. I., p. 130). Some fragments, he thinks, were pre-Mosaic; one large one as old as the beginning of Samuel's jurisdiction; another larger portion of the Pentateuch, which he calls by the name of the "Book of Origins," was composed in the reign of Solomon, but all were written three hundred years before the time of Ezra, to whose authorship the Dutch school refer a large portion of them.

It will be observed that all these scholars who had *no theories of the evolution of religious ideas* to support remit the origin of the largest portion of the Pentateuch to a very early period, and all of it to times before the reign of Josiah, 640 B.C., or two hundred years before the time of the return of Ezra. But the distinction which these scholars make between the Elohistic and Jehovistic portions of the last four books is chimerical, as will be made evident. The "archaic" style is as obvious in the Jehovistic as in the Elohistic portion; and to date the one in the time of the Judges, as Stähelin does, and the other in the time of Manasseh, five hundred years later, is a leap in literary criticism which cannot be imitated nor vindicated, and proves conclusively the falseness of these theories. Were there, therefore, no further or other evidence of the age and probable author of the Pentateuch, I should feel justified in claiming that its antiquity and authorship were as fully proved as could be reasonably expected when we consider the scant literature of these early ages and nations. But more and more conclusive proof, if possible, is waiting for admittance, derived from the writings themselves.

PART II.

INTERNAL EVIDENCE.

To APPRECIATE fully the force of the *internal evidence* which I shall present respecting the age of the Pentateuch, it is necessary to consider the circumstances under which the external evidence raises the strongest probability, if it does not prove, that it was written, and the kind of composition, both in style and construction, which under those circumstances we should expect to find.

According to the presumption raised by the external evidence and their own profession, these writings, or a large part of them, were composed during a period of forty years in which the Jewish people were sojourning in the region lying between Egypt and Palestine or Canaan. They had just escaped — a portion at least of them — as slaves from long and bitter servitude in Egypt, and were on their way to take possession of the land which their fathers had inhabited, and from which they had emigrated some hundreds of years before into Egypt. During this sojourn in the wilderness, they received laws adapted to their condition, and directing their occupation and mode of life and worship in the country of which they were to take possession. Their situation was peculiar, and peculiar regulations would be needed for both their civil and religious, as well as social, welfare. Difficulties would arise in the interpretation and execution of a new code of laws under new circumstances. Rebellions would take place when any special perils awaited the people or any disappointment overtook them. We should expect in a book composed under such circumstances that many minute incidents then occurring would be related, many laws passed, growing out of passing events, many difficulties recorded in the execution of the laws, and growing out of the contradictory character of some parts of their theoretical and experimental legislation. We should expect that the record of these years would be fragmentary, journal-like, often abrupt in its statements, disconnected, incoherent, omitting periods in which nothing specially worthy of record transpired, recording many things which have little interest to us, but which were of great importance to them. Such would be the character of the book if written under such circumstances as I have supposed, and which are affirmed in the book itself to be the circumstances in which it was composed.

Nor these marks only should we expect to find. The book would have passed through all manner of perils during the turbulent period of the judges and the establishment of the monarchy, when it had no secure place for preservation and would undoubtedly suffer in the disarrangement of its parts, the loss of some of them, the errors of any attempts at copying and correcting, the glosses of subsequent scribes to render old expressions intelligible, old names modern, old customs understood. We should expect to find, scattered all through it, the explanations, additions, queries, of more modern writers, such as the compliment to the "meekness" of Moses, the song at the old well, the modern names of old towns and old professions.

Let us now examine the books, and see whether the construction and contents of the Pentateuch do not indicate pretty clearly such an origin; whether it does not "breathe the desert air"; whether the camp and a nomadic state do not give form and coloring to the whole work; and whether the language does not contain archaic and obsolete words, and forms of words, and use words in a peculiar sense, all of which indicate a period much earlier than that in which the remaining books of the Old Testament were composed, and prove past successful refutation the Mosaic Age of the work.

SECTION I. EVIDENCE FROM STYLE AND LANGUAGE.

I will first examine the proof of its antiquity to be found in the Style and Language of the Pentateuch. Respecting "the archaisms and other peculiarities of the language" which are found in Pentateuch, De Wette says, "All that can be proved [by them] is that *some of the fragments of which it is composed are earlier than others.*" "And since the Book of Joshua, notwithstanding its affinity with Deuteronomy, does *not* possess in common with it certain archaisms, we must admit that a certain uniformity of language was observed and established by the author or compiler." * Let the reader mark two important affirmations: (1) There *are* "archaisms and other peculiarities of language" in the Pentateuch. (2) They are so marked as to distinguish even the Book of Deuteronomy from the Book of Joshua, in which they are not found. But, says De

* § 157.

Wette, "all that can be proved by these archaisms and peculiarities of language is that some of the fragments of which it [the Pentateuch] is composed are earlier than others." Now, the fact respecting these "archaisms and peculiarities" is that they are found in both the so-called Elohistic and Jehovistic documents as selected by De Wette himself. They are not limited to any of these theoretical or real documents or fragments. *They pervade the whole work.* They make as clear a distinction between the Pentateuch and all the following books of the Bible as the contents of the rocks do between the Eocene and the Miocene periods; and it is lamentable that he should have allowed himself, when struggling with this objection to his theory of the late origin of the Pentateuch, derived from its "archaisms and peculiarities of language," to entirely misrepresent the method and result of Jahn's Study on this subject. He says,* "Jahn, without examining and sifting, has huddled all together, . . . especially [names of] things which do not occur elsewhere,— technical terms." This is just what Jahn did *not* do, what he especially avoided. He omitted all such words as De Wette accuses him, in this quotation, of introducing, as our subsequent notice of Jahn's method will show. In § 34, De Wette says, "The oldest writers, the authors of the Pentateuch, . . . write in the purest and most beautiful language. . . . During the exile and after it, the influence of the Aramæan language becomes visible, as well as other peculiarities in the usage of the language." Gesenius divides Hebrew literature into two periods, that before and during and that after

* § 157, Note a.

the captivity. The "Aramæan tinges" all the second period. "The Pentateuch belongs to the first period, with Joshua and Judges and Samuel and Kings." And what is unaccountable is that, after saying that "the language and usage of the Pentateuch, in the historical passages, agree perfectly with those of the other historical books," he immediately continues: "However, the Pentateuch has some peculiarities," which he concedes may indicate "a high antiquity of these books."* Gesenius obviously means by this that they are the oldest in Hebrew literature, as the "archaisms" prove, and consequently were not written in whole or in part by Ezra. But Gesenius says more than this: "From the circumstance that these idioms appear also in the later Book of Deuteronomy, it is in the highest degree probable that a *conforming* hand has been busy with them." Mark the consequence of this "probability." Deuteronomy is supposed to be the book found or forged by Hilkiah. If so, as these critics maintain, then "the archaisms and peculiarities of language," which it is affirmed distinguish the four other books of the Pentateuch, Genesis — Numbers, had *already gone out of use*, and rendered it necessary for the writer of Deuteronomy to "*conform*" his style to those older books, in order that his forgery might escape detection. But if these books, Genesis — Numbers, were *not* written, as the Dutch school maintain, till during the captivity and after it, why was it necessary that the writer of Deuteronomy should feel compelled to "conform" his style to that of books not in existence? Indeed, to ordinary minds, it does not seem possible that he could

* De Wette, Vol. I., Appendix D, § 8.

do it without miraculous foresight. And, more wonderful still, why should these forgers of the laws during and after the captivity have taken so much pains to introduce these "archaisms and peculiarities" when there was no old literature to show that they ever existed, no older books considered sacred?

In order, however, to justify his placing Deuteronomy at a considerably later period than Genesis — Numbers, Gesenius says: "A remarkably different style prevails in Deuteronomy [from that in the earlier books]. Its most remarkable characteristic consists in a certain diffuse, rhetorical, and moralizing tone, and the constant return of favorite phrases." That is to say, "its most remarkable characteristic" is precisely that which distinguishes an oration from a statute, an address from an enactment. Deuteronomy is an oration, an address. Exodus — Numbers are made up of "orders" and "laws." They demand a different style from an address, and they have it. Yet the fragments of addresses which are scattered through these earlier books are as "diffuse, rhetorical, and moralizing in tone" as Deuteronomy. There is nothing in the *style* of Deuteronomy to separate it in age from the other books. The different styles demanded by moral precepts and statute laws and specifications for work and an address fully explain and justify the difference between the style of Exodus — Numbers and that of Deuteronomy.

Then, again, *the mood of mind* in which a person writes, and whether he dictates or holds the pen, has his extemporaneous address taken down by another or writes it out afterwards himself, make a difference in the same person's style which few critics appreciate. As I write, a notable instance of it comes to mind. It is in Mr. Whipple's *Memoir of Thomas Starr King*.* In an interview with Mr. King, Mr. Whipple says: "I maintained that he lost in compactness many of the advantages he gained in compass,— that his pen when placed in his own fingers not only hit on the best word or phrase to express his thought, but really deepened the thought by the pauses which composition exacts. The dispute culminated late one Sunday evening after he had delivered a carefully premeditated lecture on Hildebrand. I recklessly offered to distinguish among the promiscuous passages which were fresh in my memory those which he had himself written from those he had dictated to his amanuensis. Manuscript in hand, he laughingly defied me to undertake the task. By good luck, I happened to be *right in every guess*." Two thousand years hence or less, some critic of this disintegrating school will be proving to admiring students of "advanced thought" that this lecture on Hildebrand is a composite work patched up by a later hand from different authors !

As this matter of style has an important, not to say a decisive, bearing on the age of the Pentateuch, I make one more reference to the opinion of Gesenius. He says, in his *Hebrew Grammar*, Introduction, 3 : "The Pentateuch undoubtedly has some peculiarities of language which may pass for *archaisms*," and then proceeds to name a few which distinguish it from all other literature before the captivity: "Jeremiah and Ezekiel are examples of a decided approach to the Aramæan hue of the silver age," or to the books written

* Page 58.

during the later period of the captivity and after the return, "in all of which a Chaldee [Aramæan] coloring, although in different degrees, is exhibited." He says further, as quoted in Parker's *De Wette*,* " As the language appears at present in the writings of the Old Testament, we can distinguish in them only two periods distinctly marked by their character,— those writings *before* the exile and those *during the exile and after it*." On page 443, he says: "With the exile begins a *new* epoch for language and literature, which is *particularly distinguished* by an approach to the cognate East-Aramæan dialect to which the Jews in the land of exile became accustomed." And he further says, page 450: " Ezekiel stands on the borders of the two periods. . . . He shares many peculiar terms and Chaldaic expressions with his contemporary, Jeremiah. But they are more numerous in Ezekiel; and, among all writers of the Old Testament, perhaps he has proportionably the greatest number of grammatical anomalies and inaccuracies." "Ecclesiastes is tinged most deeply with Aramæan dye." This would seem to be conclusive respecting the composition of any part of the Pentateuch in this period or near it, and yet we are gravely told by Dr. Kuenen that Leviticus xviii.–xxvi. was written by this eminently Chaldeeizing Ezekiel.

Dr. Davidson says: "There are some *peculiarities* in the Pentateuch . . . which were afterwards modified or dropped. There are *diversities* between the language as found in it, and the language some centuries after, which can be recognized." " The Aramæan [Chaldee] element is a characteristic feature which distinguishes

---

* Vol. I., Appendix D, p. 440.

the language of this [later] period." "This deterioration is observable even in Jeremiah and Ezekiel, who, in point of language, stand on the borders of the two ages," that before and that after the captivity. "It is still more noticeable in the post-exile prophets."* And yet a school of critics contend that a portion of the Pentateuch was written by Ezekiel, and, more incredible still, that large parts of it were written by Ezra. Nine years later, when Davidson was goaded into becoming a partisan rather than a critic, he endeavors to parry the force of the argument derived from "archaisms" in favor of the Mosaic age of the Pentateuch by exposing the extravagant claims of some of their advocates; but he says, "We do not say that there are no diversities of language between the Pentateuch and later books." The fact then remains that there is an *observable difference in the style of the Pentateuch from that of the later books, and indicating an earlier age.* And this is all that is claimed. The more or less diversity is of no vital importance.

Ewald, the great Hebraist, whose fanciful theory of five or six writers of different portions of the Pentateuch has not been accepted by critics, says, "These fragments," referring to the earliest, according to his classification, "display *many both rare and archaic peculiarities* in the usage of words"; and he gives several in a note, and remarks, "We find here, in proportion to the trifling bulk of the passages, *a great number of words* which are either wholly unknown elsewhere, or are not usual in prose." † But the same holds true of all the portions

* *Bib. Crit.*, Vol. I., pp. 15, 18.
† *His. of Is.*, Vol. I., p. 65.

or sections made by Ewald; and these peculiarities all disappear in the books following the Pentateuch, proving that a period of considerable length must have intervened between the close of its composition and that of those books. I cannot understand how Hebrew scholars can believe that the Pentateuch, so marked by its "archaisms," could have been written after Joshua — Kings (a large part of it even by Ezra), which are free from them; and these books were most certainly written before the middle of the captivity, most of them before its commencement, and some of them as early as or earlier than the time of David.

The *emphasis* with which Ewald characterizes the difference in the style of the Pentateuch and that of the rest of the books written before the captivity (Joshua — Kings) demands notice. "The first phenomenon," he says, "that strikes the observer here is the *marked* difference in the language [of these later books] in comparison with that of the preceding great book of the primitive history [the Pentateuch]. Although both are equally made up of passages by the most diverse writers, yet on the whole *each* is distinguished by a *peculiar* cast of language. Many fresh words and expressions become favorites here [in Joshua — Kings] and supplant their equivalents in the primitive history [Genesis — Deuteronomy]; others that are *thoroughly in vogue* here [in Joshua — Kings] are ... avoided in the primitive history. But the *most remarkable and pervading characteristic* is that words of common life, which *never* occur to the pen of any single relater of the primitive history, find an *unquestioned* reception here [in Joshua — Kings]." "I have no hesitation in saying," he yet more emphatically affirms, "that the *established usage of centuries* must have sanctioned for the primitive history [the Pentateuch] a style of narrative and a cast of language *utterly different* from those customary in the history of the Kings," in which Ewald includes Judges — Kings. They "naturally created a *new style* of narrative and of language."* The italics are mine. Ewald here affirms that for "centuries" the "primitive style" of the Pentateuch existed before the writers of the later books and literature lived. But we have good reason to believe that we have remains of literature as early as the time of David in some of the Psalms, to say nothing of the probability that the Book of Judges and portions of Samuel and all of Joshua may have been written in his reign or shortly after, in none of which are there any of the "archaisms and peculiarities of language" which are "*utterly different* from those customary" in Joshua — Kings, and constituting a "*new style* of narrative and language." But, according to the estimate of many modern critics, only about three centuries intervened between Moses and David or Solomon, and only about five, according to the earlier critics. Ewald's "usage of centuries" reaches back easily to the time of Moses in either chronology. To make as great a change in the language as he affirms, that length of time, in that age, would be required. The age of the Pentateuch is thrown back, therefore, to the time of Moses by the demand of its "*utterly different*" style from that of the later books. For this "archaic style tinges" *all the different documents* of which some critics think the work is composed, as Ewald admits "even Deuteronomy to be."†

* Vol. I., pp. 134, 135. † Page 135.

These opinions of eminent Hebrew scholars, with which nine-tenths of the scholars in this country who can read Hebrew agree, must suffice as proof of the "archaic style" of the Pentateuch. A popular essay like this is not the place for a minute exhibition and criticism of these "archaisms and peculiarities of language." A few specimens only will be given, as indications of their character, and illustrations of their number and variety, in which the common reader may be interested.

The most striking and obvious peculiarity in the style of the Pentateuch is the use of the same word for the singular pronoun in the third person of both genders, *he* and *she*. In the rest of the Hebrew writings, a distinction is always made and a different word is used for the feminine pronoun *she*. Ewald himself admits that "this is a proof which cannot be mistaken, in favor of the *high* antiquity of the Pentateuch." And when we remember that this pronoun is used nearly two hundred times in the Pentateuch, and, with but eleven exceptions, in the same form, the "proof" becomes decisive that the book is older than any other Hebrew writings which have come down to us; hence older even than the Psalms of David, in which no such "archaic" word is found. The same remark may be made respecting a word which in the Pentateuch is used *twenty-five* times, and is applied indifferently to either a young man or a young woman; while in the other Hebrew writings the feminine termination is added to distinguish the gender. A peculiar form of the plural demonstrative pronoun "these" is found in the Pentateuch. One phrase which indicates strongly the very early origin of the book is that used to denote the death of an Israelite. He is said "to be gathered *to his people*"; while in the later writings he is said "to be gathered *to his fathers*." The nation not yet being settled in the land of promise, the "fathers" are not spoken of. A peculiar word is used in the Pentateuch to denote *species*, *kind*, of animals and plants twenty-eight times, and is *never* used in later writings, with but one exception, when Ezekiel (xlvii., 10) most obviously quotes the language of the Pentateuch, Genesis i., 21. A peculiar phrase is used twenty-one times to signify the relation of the sexes. Fourteen times a peculiar word is used for *lamb*. A peculiar word for *laugh* is used thirteen times, or rather a peculiar spelling of a word. A peculiar word is used fifty times for *goat* which is *never* used for that animal in the other books. A word is used for *female* twenty-one times in the Pentateuch, and never in the other writings except by Jeremiah (xxxi., 22), with evident reference to the old usage. *Nephesh* is used eighteen times for "creature" and but once elsewhere, Ezekiel xlvii., 9. Such is a specimen of the "archaic" words and phrases used in this book. Dr. Jahn, who made a special examination of these "archaisms," after omitting all words which treat of subjects peculiar to the Pentateuch, such as names of towns, villages, nations, men; of diseases and symptoms of diseases; of blemishes in sacrifices, priests, men, and women; of parts of the tabernacle, and its altars, curtains, and furniture,— in short, after the omission of *all* words which were used to signify things or ideas *not* spoken of in the later books,— found *over two hundred words, used from two to two hundred times each, which are peculiar to the Pentateuch.** When we consider the meagre vocabulary of Hebrew words, this number is a very large one, and is conclusive evidence that the book was composed in a period remote from that in which the other Hebrew books were written. "The few solitary Chaldaisms which occur in the writings of the Golden Age," and which have been adduced as proof of the modern origin of the Pentateuch, Gesenius says, "may be accounted for by the fact that these books passed through the hands of copyists whose language was Chaldee." Besides, it is not certain that all these so-called Chaldaisms are such. "Some of them are not found," says Gesenius, "in Chaldee, and seem to have belonged to the Hebrew popular dialect." †

Looking at the language only, therefore, we are required to refer the Pentateuch to an age as remote as that of Moses. It is objected, however, to this view of the age of the Pentateuch, that the language must have undergone a *greater* change between the

---

* Yet in the face of all this conscientious and scholarly discrimination, De Wette is rash enough and unjust enough to say that Jahn was utterly heedless and undiscriminating in his selection of words.

† The latest statement which I have seen respecting the language of the Pentateuch is contained in a notice of a *Historico-Critical Commentary on the Language of the Elohist in the Pentateuch* (by C. Victor Ryssel: 8vo, pp. 92; Leipzig, Fernan, 1878), in which it is said that "the result of the author's laborious examinations is that *only some parts* of the Books of Exodus, Leviticus, Numbers, contain peculiarities of language which point to a *rather late* date of composition. These are the parts which, taken together, form the so-called Priest's Code. But the *greater* parts of the Elohistic book, and the weightiest, *i.e.*, the historic and the supreme laws, are to be referred to the *early* days of the literature of the Israelite people." Of the ability of this scholar to decide on this subject, I have no knowledge. Accepting his decision as correct respecting the fact of "certain peculiarities of language" in the ritual which "point to a rather late date of composition," this would be expected; for ritual language survives all other, and would be used, when ritualistic matters were treated of, long centuries after the ritual was composed and adopted.

Mosaic Age, in which it is claimed that the Pentateuch was written, and the age in which the remaining books, Joshua — Kings, were written, than we find that it has undergone in these books. If, however, Joshua and Judges and a portion of Samuel were written in the age of David or Solomon, as is most probable, only about three hundred years intervened between their composition and that of the Pentateuch, according to the most commonly received chronology; and, setting their composition as late as that of the Books of the Kings, but about seven hundred years separate them. Now, it is well known that the early Oriental languages do not change as rapidly as those in modern days. The late George H. Smith, the eminent Assyriologist, says: * "The texts of Rim-agu, Sargon, Hammurali, who were one thousand years before Nebuchadnezzar and Nabonidus, show the same language as the texts of these later kings, there being no sensible difference in style to match the long interval between them." These older texts were of the age of Moses, according to the old chronology, and just as much time elapsed between their composition and the later texts as elapsed between the time of Moses and the captivity, when the Books of the Kings were written; but, according to the new chronology, the text of Rim-agu is three hundred years older than that of the Pentateuch.

The Egyptologists also testify to the slight changes which took place in the early centuries in the language of Egypt. In the *Revue Archéologique* (1867, unless my reference is incorrect) is the following statement: " In comparing the demotic papyrus with the romance of

* Vol. II., p. 23.

the Two Brothers, even a superficial examination shows, not only that the language and the formulæ of the two papyri, separated from each other by an interval of some thousand years, are of the same kind, but also — a point of most special interest — even the grammar has not undergone the least change." Well might there not have been any greater change in the Hebrew language of the time of Moses down to the time of the captivity than we find when we compare the language of the Pentateuch and that of the Books of the Kings. There is a change, and as great as we should expect to find under the circumstances, as great as the analogy of other Oriental languages would lead us to anticipate.

The language of the Pentateuch is "archaic"; signally different from the earliest of the other writings, and some of these date back to the time of David. The time between Moses and David was none too great to have wrought this difference. Governed by the language of the work, we must date the Pentateuch as early as the Mosaic Age.

Nor can it be said with any ground of reason that this "archaic language" in the Pentateuch is only the "priestly idiom" which was used by the priestly forgers, Hilkiah and Ezra; for there is no proof that there was any "priestly idiom." And, more than this, the writings of the priests which have come down to us contain none of these "archaic peculiarities." Jeremiah, Ezekiel, Ezra, Haggai, Zechariah, all priests, write in the degenerate language of the age of the captivity, and use none of the "archaic" words which distinguish the language of the Pentateuch from all the other books. This they would not have done, had these peculiar words been the special vocabulary of priestly men.

Before dismissing a consideration of the language of the Pentateuch, as furnishing an argument for its antiquity, it is necessary to consider an objection to this conclusion which has been drawn from the marked diversity of style in the books themselves. A sufficient reply to this objection, so far as my argument is concerned, is that, however diverse the style of the different parts of these books may be, the style of *all these parts* is "archaic," and hence they were written long before Joshua — Kings. But I cannot admit that such diversities of style as the objection implies are found in the Pentateuch. Excepting the first eleven chapters of Genesis, which contain some notices of the world before the time of Abraham, and excepting several passages in the remainder of Genesis, there is a unity of style as clearly marked as in any writing by even one person, spread over as long a period (forty years) and including as many different subjects, to say nothing of the probability of the employment of scribes who would naturally write in different styles while using the same "archaic language." I have gone through the drudgery of examining all De Wette's divisions founded upon what he is pleased to call diversities of style, and have risen from the task entirely satisfied that there is no good foundation for any such wide diversities as he maintains are to be found, making it possible with any degree of certainty to identify the different writers. The self-contradictory nature of some of the rules by which he professes to be governed, the different words which in different sections he quotes as proving the identity of the authorship of some sections and the different authorship of other sections, are sufficient to lead the student to suspect that a mistake has been made in this portion of his Introduction; and upon further and closer examination he will find his suspicions changed into firm conclusions that such heterogeneousness of style, as is affirmed so decidedly to exist, is not to be found in these books. But we will not be allured much further from a positive consideration of our subject by the fruitful field of criticism which opens before us in this direction.

A very brief space only must be taken to illustrate the fatuity of all such attempts to cull out the parts which are attributed to the different hypothetical writers. I use De Wette's fragments, who confesses to following "Stähelin's plan." Did De Wette test this plan by comparing it with the text? It does not seem possible. He says Exodus xvi. is from the Elohist writer, yet God is called *Elohim* but once and *Jehovah* twenty-two times. Chapter xx., 19-21, is Jehovistic, and yet God is called Elohim three times and not once Jehovah. Leviticus iii., 6, is called Elohistic, yet God is called Jehovah. These are selected as Elohistic, yet God is called Jehovah in all of them: Leviticus vi., 18; vii., 20, 21; x., 15, used twice. Leviticus xiv., Jehovah is used twenty-three times, Elohim once. Leviticus i.-iii., Jehovah twenty-nine times, Elohim once; xvii., 4-10, Jehovah seven times, Elohim not once; xix., 8, 34, Jehovah in each; xxii., 3, Jehovah twice; xxiv., 16, 22, Jehovah in both; xxvii., 9, 11, 16, 21, 22, 28, Jehovah eight times and Elohim not once in these later references. Let us look into Numbers i.-x.: Jehovah is used ninety-nine times, Elohim *once!* xviii., Jehovah sixteen times, Elohim not once; xx., 1-13, Jehovah seven times, Elohim once; xxv., 1-18, Jehovah six times, Elohim once. These are sufficient illustrations of the complete unreliableness of this attempt to parcel out these books, Exodus — Numbers, among different authors on this use of the names of God. Further exposure was made of the attempt in the Review of Kuenen, p. 71.*

* The utter futility of all attempts to separate the Levitical or priestly parts of the middle books, Exodus — Numbers, from the rest of the writing, will be best understood by the reader from the disagreements of the scholars who have attempted to separate them. I will give the parts selected by Nöldeke, as quoted by Prof. Smith, pp. 442, 443, and as selected by Stähelin, as quoted in Parker's De Wette, Vol. II., pp. 106-130.

For greater ease in comparing them, I will tabulate their selections. The verses selected are often not connected.

Exodus, chapter		i.,	Nöldeke	9 verses;	"	Stähelin	22
"	"	ii.,	"	2½	"	"	3
"	"	vi.,	"	27	"	"	30
"	"	vii.,	"	15½	"	"	7
"	"	viii.,	"	7½	"	"	0
"	"	ix.,	"	5	"	"	0
"	"	xi.,	"	2	"	"	0
"	"	xii.,	"	37	"	"	42
"	"	xiii.,	"	3	"	"	4
"	"	xiv.,	"	15 3-2	"	"	0
"	"	xv.,	"	2½	"	"	0
"	"	xvi.,	"	36	"	"	15
"	"	xvii.,	"	16	"	"	0
"	"	xix.,	"	2	"	"	0
"	"	xx.-xxiv.,	"	3	"	"	118*
"	"	xxi.-xxxi., 17	"	all	"	"	all
"	"	xxxv.-xl.,	"	all	"	"	all
Leviticus, "		i.-xxvi., 2	"	all but 48	"	"	all
"	"	xxvii.,	"	all	"	"	all†
Numbers, "		i.-viii., 22	"	all	"	"	4 verses more
"	"	ix.-x., 28	"	all	"	"	9 verses more
"	"	xiii.,	"	19 3-2	"	"	all

* De Wette and Parker differ from both Nöldeke and Stähelin and from each other.
† Parker utterly objects to both.

I cannot close this already extended discussion of the "archaic language" of the Pentateuch as proof of its high antiquity, without saying that my reading of the Hebrew and my examination of the discussion of the eminent critics quoted above compel me to make *three* periods of the language of the Old Testament Scriptures: The first covering the Pentateuch; the second, Joshua — Kings; the third, Chronicles — Esther. The poetical books belonging to the second and third periods can be nearly as easily distinguished as the historical.

Numbers, chapter		xiv.,	Nöldeke	23 verses;	Stähelin		all
"	"	xvi.,	"	7 3-2	"	"	all
"	"	xvii.-xix.,	"	all	"	"	confused
"	"	xx.,	"	18½	"	"	confused
"	"	xxi.,	"	2½	"	"	0
"	"	xxii.,	"	1	"	"	0
"	"	xxv.,	"	18	"	"	0
"	"	xxvi.,	"	53½	"	"	65
"	"	xxvii.,	"	all	"	"	all
"	"	xxviii.,	"	0	"	"	all
"	"	xxix.,	"	0	"	"	all
"	"	xxx.,	"	14	"	"	16
"	"	xxxi.,	"	all	"	"	all
"	"	xxxii.,	"	23½	"	"	32
"	"	xxxiii.,	"	50	"	"	49
"	" xxxiv.-xxxvi.,	"	all	"	"	all

Decided dissent is expressed by both De Wette and Parker from many of these selections, which I did not think it necessary to note. Prof. Smith says, "Nöldeke's table is generally accepted as careful and *correct in essentials*." De Wette says, "Stähelin's is, as a whole, *certainly correct!*" The italics are mine. Comment is unnecessary. But that the reader may see what this table does not show, the *manner* in which these verses are selected by Nöldeke, I will give a few specimens as furnishing farther proof of the imaginary line which separates the verses chosen and the verses left. Exodus i., 1-5, 7, 13, 14; ii., 23, 24, 25; xiii., 1, 2, 20; xii., 1-23, 28, 37, 40-51; xi., 9, 10; Numbers xvi., 1, half of 2, 3-11, 16-23, part of 24, 26, 27, 35; xxxii., 2 (3?), 4-6, 16-32, part of 33, 40. These specimens must suffice. Any reader can turn to the Bible, and judge whether there is any ground for selecting just these passages. I have no fear of the result.

SECTION II. EVIDENCE FROM CONTENTS AND STRUCTURE.

Were there, therefore, no other evidence of the age of the composition of the Pentateuch, its archaic language would be sufficient to determine it. But there is other evidence corroborative of this, and also adding its own independent weight to the same conclusion. This evidence is found in the *contents* and *structure* of the books of the Pentateuch, and determines their age as certainly and as evidently as the contents and structure of the rocks determine their age. The contents and structure of the Silurian rocks no more surely prove their deposition to have been before the Devonian than the contents and structure of the Pentateuch prove it to have been written before any other books in the Bible.

Another internal argument in favor of the antiquity of the Pentateuch is found in the *journal-like* character of the work itself. It is in precisely the form it would have been in, had it been written under the circumstances commonly believed to exist at the time of its composition. It is fragmentary and abrupt, relating incidents in such a manner and form as to induce the belief that the writer was on the spot and narrated what he saw, and his own feelings under the circumstances. To fully appreciate this characteristic of the Pentateuch, or the last four books of it, we must go into particulars, which will show very clearly that they were composed on the spot where the transactions recorded transpired.

I. I will first refer to the occurrence of *unexpected difficulties* which arose, making it necessary to amend or repeal laws which had been previously enacted. A marked instance of this nature occurs respecting the law of inheritance in accordance with which none but *sons* could inherit the real estate of the father; and specific regulations were made respecting the manner in which it should be divided. But, when the tribes were about to enter upon possession of the promised land, the daughters of Zelophehad came forward, and stated that their father had left no sons at his death, and therefore that their father's portion of the land would go out of the family. They pray, therefore, that a possession may be given them among their brethren. To meet this emergency, Moses enacts a new, or rather amends the old, law. He enacts that, "if a man die and have no son, then ye shall cause his inheritance to pass unto his daughter." And farther provisions are made in case no daughter should survive (Numbers xxvi., 1–11). If we turn forward nine chapters, we shall find that this new law was found to be as defective as the old one, but in another direction. It was the intention of Moses that no part of the inheritance of one tribe should pass into the possession of another tribe. But these daughters of Zelophehad were proposing to marry into another tribe,— not into that to which their father belonged. This caused the children of the other families of the tribe to make complaint to Moses that his amendment to the old law, which gave the inheritance to the sons only, and giving it, in case of no sons, to the daughters, would disinherit their *tribe* of a part of their estate, since these daughters of Zelophehad were about to marry out of the tribe, and thus take their father's inheritance with them. Moses saw the conflicting nature of both the original law and his amendment, and he *amended the amendment* by enacting that, in all cases, "every daughter that possesseth an inheritance in any tribe of the children of Israel shall be wife unto one of the family of the tribe of her father, that the children of Israel may enjoy every man the inheritance of his fathers." Let, therefore, the daughters of Zelophehad "marry to whom they think best; only to the family of the tribe of their fathers shall they marry" (Numbers xxxvi.). Thus, after *three* experiments, the law is perfected, and the details of the cause of these changes are given *as if written on the spot*. Would a compiler of the laws of the Hebrews in the time of Ezra have thus stated this matter? It is very improbable, not to say incredible.

Another incident is related, showing the imperfect character of the first enactment, and how, from time to time, laws were added to meet these new emergencies. A man was found violating the Sabbath by picking up sticks (Numbers xv., 32). The law had forbidden all work. A man is found violating the law: *how* is he to be punished? Moses adds a new section to the law containing the penalty for violating the Sabbath. Stone him with stones without the camp. Here we see clearly that a history of the origin of the penalty is given, which would not have been given by a compiler of a later age. The same is true of the law against blasphemy (Leviticus xxiv., 10-23) to be noticed soon.

The change which was made in the law respecting *usury* indicates the journal-like character of the Pentateuch. It is first enacted (Exodus xxii., 25) that no usury shall be taken of the *poor*, as it would be oppressive;

but it is distinctly implied that it might be taken of the rich. Just as the tribes were to enter Canaan, thirty-eight years after, we find that this law is so modified as to forbid the taking of usury from *any* Hebrew (Deuteronomy xxiii., 19). It had been found, probably, that very little money would be loaned to the poor without usury, when it could be loaned to the rich with usury. *All usury of Hebrews is therefore now forbidden.* But another curious change is found in these usury laws respecting strangers who came to dwell among the Hebrews. Soon after the people left Egypt, it was enacted that no usury should be taken of the poor of their own people, but of the poor of other people who had come among them nothing is said. In about two years, just before the people leave Sinai, a more stringent law is passed respecting usury (Leviticus xxv., 35); and strangers are included in it, and especially those who had been overtaken by calamity and had lost their property. Just before entering Canaan (Deuteronomy xxiii., 19), we find that the law forbidding usury when loans were made to sojourners and strangers is repealed. It is very easy to see why a writer on the spot should insert all these particulars; but it is not easy to see why a later writer giving a compend of the law should have inserted all these minute matters, or indeed how he could have known them unless some one had written them at the time, and the later writer had used his journal. The old law was found upon trial to be imperfect: an amendment was enacted, and inserted in the book containing the legislative proceedings, as is done at this day.

An unforeseen difficulty arose respecting the passover

(Leviticus xxiii., 1). *Every* Israelite was bound by the original law to keep the passover on the *fourteenth* day of the *first* month, and a heavy penalty rested upon him who failed to obey it. Yet it was equally perilous for a person ritually unclean to minister in any sacred rite. In Numbers ix., we have the record of such a conflict in the laws. "Certain men who were defiled by the dead body of a man," so that they could not keep the passover, came to Moses and Aaron and inquired what they should do. Moses saw the conflict in the laws, and enacted that they, and all persons who should hereafter be in their situation, might eat the passover on the *fourteenth* day of the *second* month, regarding, at the same time, all the ceremonies which were required of those who ate it in the previous month.

A long series of amendments is found in Deuteronomy to adapt laws, many of which were designed for a camp and nomadic life, to the settled, agricultural condition of the people in Canaan. In camp, they were required to kill their animals for food at the tabernacle, that the priests might see that no idolatrous rites were performed with the blood and entrails: in the land of their inheritance, they could kill animals for food at their own homes. Tents were to be exchanged for houses, and laws respecting their construction and purification are enacted.

A difficulty arose respecting the penalty to be inflicted on one of that "mixed" race which came out of Egypt with Israel. A son of an Israelitish woman and of a man of Egypt had a fray, blasphemed and cursed. He is kept in ward till his case could be inquired into, and it is at last determined, after careful inquiry, that he should be put to death as an Israelite must be who had committed the same crime (Leviticus xxiv., 10–23). Such changes, additions, and amendments in the laws, made to meet emergencies apparently unforeseen, most certainly indicate a writer on the spot, and not a historian of remotely succeeding generations.

II. But this Book of Deuteronomy and the light which it throws upon the age of the Pentateuch demand a thorough examination, as so much misapprehension exists concerning both.

Dr. Kuenen affirms that the forger of Deuteronomy *intended to deceive the people*, and that "men used to perpetrate such fictions without any qualms of conscience."* De Wette says: "The author of Deuteronomy would have us regard his whole book as the work of Moses" (Parker's *De Wette*, Vol. II., p. 159). Davidson says, "A late writer represents the whole of Deuteronomy, or at least chapters iv., 44–xxx., as proceeding from Moses' hand." ... "The deception was an innocent one, being merely a veil or *form* for communicating and enforcing lessons of importance!" Indeed, all supporters of this theory admit that Deuteronomy is a *flagrant forgery*. Yet they are compelled to admit, also, that the writer had before him many older documents containing laws ancient and venerated. I propose to show how the laws given at Sinai, forty years before, were amended on the east bank of the Jordan by the original law-giver, and thus prove by its contents that the address of Moses is not a "fiction" written eight centuries later, but a substan-

* Vol. II., p. 18.

tially correct report of a real transaction. In Deuteronomy xii.–xxvi., we have a series of additions and amendments to previous laws, *all based upon new circumstances or defects discovered in the original enactment,* none of them affecting the fundamental law of the nation. It would require more space than I can take, and more patience in the reader than can be assumed, to quote or refer to all the changes made and the reasons for them; nor is it necessary for my argument to do so. A few must suffice as indicating the rest. I give the following as average illustrations of all of them: Permission is given to the people to kill animals at their own homes instead of at the door of the tabernacle. Secretly enticing to idolatry is made a capital crime. Idolatrous cities are to be razed to the ground. Mourners are not to shave between the eyes. A dead carcass may be sold to an alien. The animals that may be eaten are named. When the distance is "too great to carry the tithe of corn and wine and oil and the firstlings of thy herds and flocks" to the place which God shall choose, "then thou shalt turn it into money" to use at the place chosen. Payment of debts is not to be enforced in the Sabbatical year from the poor. Slaves are to be emancipated on the seventh year. Female slaves are to have the same rights as males: they are to be provided for, when bearing, by their master. Judges are to be appointed in all cities. Regulations are made respecting a king. An addition is made to a priest's perquisites. A test of a false prophet is given. Minute regulations are made respecting cities of refuge. Landmarks are not to be changed. Two witnesses are to be required for "any iniquity" as well as for "murder." A false witness is to be punished as the criminal, if guilty, would be. Regulations are given for drafting soldiers for war. Trees are not to be destroyed when besieging cities. The treatment of a town in case of uncertain murder is described. Conditions of marrying a female captive are given, etc. There are over *sixty amendments and additions* to the law as contained in Exodus — Numbers, in these chapters, and they are such as one having the original laws before him would, under the circumstances, have made; but it appears incredible that one having the laws of Deuteronomy before him could have composed those of Exodus — Numbers, as the theory assumes.

Again, the indirect quotations of the original laws and references to them contained in Exodus — Numbers, by the speaker in Deuteronomy, in connection with the amendments and additions which he makes, are of such a kind as to compel the belief that Exodus — Numbers were in the hand of the speaker; at any rate, they raise a violent presumption that these books were already written, and their contents well known to the Deuteronomist.

In about a dozen places, the speaker in Deuteronomy quotes from what God "had commanded" or "said," and his quotation or reference is found in the previous books. In some instances, the quotations are verbal; in others, free, but including a peculiar word or phrase, as not to "lift up" an iron tool on building an altar (Deuteronomy xxvii., 5 = Exodus xx., 26); to drive out the Canaanites "little by little" (Deuteronomy vii., 22 = Exodus xxiii., 30); God is a "jealous God"

(Deuteronomy iv., 24=Exodus xx., 5); thou shalt not wear a garment of "divers sorts" (Deuteronomy xxii., 11=Leviticus xix., 9). Some of these words and phrases are used only in the passages quoted. These quotations are sufficient to indicate the character of the rest of the passages, and the reader can judge of their weight in this argument. To an unbiassed critic who had no theory to support, they alone would seem to be decisive of the whole question. But lest some readers should still hesitate to accept this conclusion on the testimony of these passages, I will trespass upon the patience of others by quoting a few more passages which must remove the least shadow of doubt. In Deuteronomy i., 16–18, Moses says the "judges shall not respect persons in judgment, but ye shall hear the small as well as great, and judge righteously between every man and his brother. . . . I *commanded you at that time* ['whilst at Horeb'] all the things which ye should do." In Leviticus xix., 15, is the original law. In Deuteronomy iii., 18, Moses says, addressing the tribes which were to settle on the east side of Jordan, "I *commanded you at that time*, saying, Ye shall pass over armed before your brethren," and help them subdue the land first. This command is in Numbers xxxii., 20–23. In Deuteronomy xi., 22–25, in order to encourage the people to go up and take the land, Moses reminds them that the "Lord *hath said* that he will drive out all these nations from before you." This saying of the Lord is in Exodus xxiii., 27–29. In Deuteronomy xviii., 2, he says, "The tribe of Levi . . . shall have no inheritance among their brethren; the Lord is their inheritance, *as* *he hath said* unto them"; and he said it in Numbers xviii., 20. In Deuteronomy xx., 17, Moses repeats the "command of the Lord" contained in Exodus xxxiv., 11, to drive out or exterminate the "Hittites and the Amorites, the Canaanites and the Perizzites, the Hivites and the Jebusites," from the land. In Deuteronomy xxiv., 8, Moses directs the people "to take heed in the plague of leprosy to observe diligently and do according to all that the priests the Levites shall teach you; as I *commanded* these, so ye shall observe to do." This "command" is found in Leviticus xiii., 14.*

* A writer in the *Unitarian Review*, October, 1880, p. 303, after reciting the stoning of Achan's children, with their father, for his sin, and the hanging of seven of Saul's sons for the sin of Saul in slaying the Gibeonites, says, "If they had had the law of Deuteronomy, 'The children shall not be put to death for the father,'" Joshua would not "have killed Achan's innocent children," nor David "have hanged the seven innocent sons of Saul." Perhaps they were no better interpreters of the Law of Moses than the Supreme Court of the United States, headed by the profound Chief Justice Taney, when he said, "The negroes had no rights which a white man was bound to respect"; and, possibly, the apparent conflict of laws may have puzzled the poorly educated jurists, Joshua and David, for the so-called ten tables announced that their God was "a jealous God, *visiting the iniquity of the fathers upon the children unto the third and fourth* generation of them that hate him." If, under the light of the nineteenth century, the highest court in the United States could announce such an opinion as Chief Justice Taney's, may not Joshua have been mistaken three thousand years before? More remarkable still, two *opposite decisions* were made by the same court within about a year, touching a more vital point in the Constitution,— the constitutionality of the legal-tender law raising paper money to an equality with gold. Different interpretations of a law are so far from proving that there is no law that they prove its existence past all question.

It may not be inapposite to remind the reader that different interpretations are very frequently given of law by different administrations, and that laws for generations obsolete or remaining unenforced are revived and enforced, as just at this time the English law of eviction, which has been obsolete for two centuries, is being enforced in Ireland, or as an old law of Maryland has just been discovered, which requires the tongue of a Unitarian, one who denies the Trinity, to be bored through with an iron, which never was enforced and whose existence surprises the present generation.

He also objects that two different reasons would not have been given for keeping

But I must refrain from quoting further. Reasonable readers have rights which unreasonable ones are bound to respect. If these passages are not conclusive and do not remove the last shadow of a reasonable doubt, then the presence and testimony of Moses himself could not dispel it. The author of Deuteronomy was familiar with the preceding books, or historical questions are incapable of settlement.

So evident are these references, and so numerous, that even Dr. Davidson admits that "it is possible that the *successive laws* may have been given by Moses,

the Sabbath in Deuteronomy v. and Exodus xx. by the so-called Originist, the former because of release from Egyptian bondage, the latter because of God's rest from creating. But would the Originist writing *after* the Deuteronomist, with whose reason he was familiar and the people also, and which would be so pleasant to them, have given another and obviously much less touching and humane reason?

The same writer affirms that Deuteronomy and the historical books take a wholly different view of the sacerdotal tribe and the priesthood from Exodus — Numbers (*Unitarian Review*, p. 307). He says that in Joshua — Kings the restriction to sacrifice to the family of Aaron is unknown. This objection has been fully answered in the text. In some cases the law may have been violated by supposed necessity, in others priests may have been officiators, but not named. *Quid facit per alium facit per se*; and so far is it from being true, as this writer affirms, that Ezekiel is the parent of the priestly legislation, that he is perpetually referring to and quoting the laws relating to sacrifices already in existence, as I have most fully illustrated.

The same writer affirms in italics, on page 305, that the "Deuteronomist is unacquainted with the Book of Origins," or the main portion of the other books of the Pentateuch, and appeals to Deuteronomy xii., 8, and Leviticus xiv., 8, 9, to prove it. In Deuteronomy, referring to the change in their condition consequent on the people's passing over Jordan, the writer says, "Ye shall not do after all the things that we do here this day, every man whatsoever is right in his own eyes," — that is, regarding the law as best you can in your migratory condition. But, in Leviticus, the Originist, so called, says that he who regardeth not the law of sacrifice referred to "shall be cut off from among his people." But if the Originist wrote *after* the Deuteronomist, as is maintained, would he have written that it was a law given on the mount to Moses by Jehovah, when the Deuteronomist had written that there was no such law in existence according to these interpreters?

from the first code at Sinai till the time of his death in Moab; the legislation being supplemented, enlarged, modified, altered as circumstances arose."* And he also admits, respecting Deuteronomy, that "it is possible indeed to conceive of Moses, provided he wrote the preceding books of the Pentateuch, giving a survey of the historical circumstances through which he had passed at the head of the Israelites, and modifying or abrogating such enactments as would be unsuitable to the people when they had obtained possession of the promised land." † "There is no doubt," he says, "that it [Deuteronomy] is built on the historical facts embodied in the former parts of the Pentateuch. It alludes to them throughout. Yet it is still possible . . . that his [the author's] acquaintance with them may have been borrowed from *oral tradition*." But, only two pages further on, Dr. Davidson says: "These proofs [filling three pages] of the Deuteronomist's acquaintance with the four preceding books might be multiplied, since *almost every chapter* presents some indication, however slight, that *written* documents were employed by him." ‡ Now pass on seven pages further, and we find Dr. Davidson saying, "The Deuteronomist found the first four books *made up in their present form* of two or more leading documents, and terminating with Moses' death." Comment on such criticism is unnecessary. Dr. Kuenen, who maintains that the chief portion of Exodus — Numbers was not composed till two centuries *after* Deuteronomy, must settle the matter as he can with Dr. Davidson, who affirms that the "four books," Genesis

---

* Vol. I., p. 75. † Vol. I., p. 253.
‡ Vol. I., pp. 386, 387. The italics are mine.

—Numbers, "in their present form," were in the hands of the Deuteronomist.

III. Another evidence of the time and place and manner of writing these books and enacting these laws is found in Deuteronomy xxviii.–xxx. compared with Leviticus xxvi. At the conclusion of the residence at Sinai, when the code and ritual had been given, Moses exhorts the people, Leviticus xxvi., to obedience, as they were soon to be settled in the promised land, by all the motives which could influence a patriotic and religious people. He pictures before them all the blessings of peace and all the luxuries of prosperity consequent upon obedience, and all the desolations of war and the horrors of famine and plague which will follow disobedience. It was as natural as fit that then and there such an earnest and ardent and admonitory address should be made. But the people did not enter the land as was expected. They wandered about for thirty-eight years, till nearly all who heard the address had forgotten it or were dead. We are not surprised, therefore, to find, as the people were about to enter the land after their long wanderings, and as their great leader could not pass over with them, that he again addresses them at even greater length and with supreme earnestness. The same principles are clothed in more glowing language, and are warmed with a patriot's anxiety and importunity. The time, the circumstances, give coloring to the words spoken. Accept the historical account as correct, and both speeches find their place and justification. Deny the reliableness of the history, and either the one or the other of the speeches is superfluous, and its origin cannot be accounted for, nor the location of the one in the Book of Leviticus justified. The internal evidence of the age and origin of the Pentateuch, derived from the construction, contents, and repeated references to the other books, and the amendments and repeal of laws contained in them, the enactment of new laws demanded by the changed conditions of the people, as exhibited in Deuteronomy, would of itself justify the belief of the Mosaic Age of these books.

But there is more evidence of the same kind contained in the description of the condition of the people, and the enactment of new laws, and the amendment of old ones, thirty-seven years before, when the people were about to enter Canaan from Kadesh, as written in the Book of Numbers to which we must now turn our attention.*

IV. The fourteenth chapter of Numbers closes apparently the account of the residence of the people at Kadesh after the repulse of the revolutionary attempt to force their way into Canaan. No further account is given of them till they appear again at Kadesh in the desert of Zin, thirty-seven years afterwards. Of this period, we know nothing except the list of stations where they encamped, given in the thirty-third chapter, and the modified or new laws, given in chapters xv.–xix., including the rebellion of Korah. I propose now to examine these chapters to see what light they throw upon the age and authorship of the Pentateuch.

These regulations were made with express reference to

---

* A writer in the *Unitarian Review*, October, 1880, page 302, says: "The Deuteronomist could not have known the Levitical law as we now have it. . . . He flatly contradicts many of its most positive statements." The repeal of some of the old laws and the enactment of different ones, as shown above, rather proves a familiarity with them.

the wants of people when settled in the promised land, and when they were supposed to be about to enter it. "When ye come into the land of your habitations," says Moses, you will regard the following laws. As the history records, it was supposed by Moses as well as by the people that they were to enter at once upon their inheritance; and therefore he had so improved the original code as to better adapt it to their new condition. There is no reason to suppose he would have made these additions and amendments, as recorded in the fifteenth chapter, now, if he had known they were to be wanderers in the wilderness one generation, or thirty-seven years longer. The history implies the reason why these laws were made *then*, and the implication of immediate entrance "into their habitations" contained in the publication of such laws confirms the authenticity of the history, and shows the journal-like style of the work. The fifteenth chapter was written evidently *before* the repulse took place, and the rebellion was punished by the denial of that generation to enter the land.

Do the laws themselves, as compared with other laws, throw any light upon the origin of these books? Chapter xv., 1-16, extends the regulation respecting strangers at the passover to all the sacrificial ritual, as if the people were to be so situated that strangers would be very likely to join them more frequently than they had done before; and, most obviously, strangers would be more numerous when they were settled in the land. Again, the quantity of flour and oil and wine is specified for each offering of a lamb or of a ram or of a bullock, as if there would be hereafter no lack of flour and oil and wine as there was in the desert, when the quantity for an offering was not specified (Leviticus ii.),— indicating that they were about to change a nomadic for an agricultural life.

Numbers xv., 17–21. This law of the "heave offering" of a "cake of the first of the dough," with grain taken from the "*threshing floor*," is *new*, and implies that they were soon to be husbandmen. No such ceremony of thankfulness could have been observed in the desert.

Numbers xv., 22–29. "A kid of the goats" is added to the sin-offering for sins of ignorance of the congregation (Leviticus iv., 13–21). The cause of this addition does not appear. But emphasis is laid on the obligation of "the stranger that sojourneth" with them to obey this law, as if more such persons would be likely to be among them. This is new. Numbers xv., 30–36. The presumptuous sinner is to "be cut off from among his people"; and a case of such presumptuous violation of the law of observing the Sabbath is brought before Moses, and he decides that the *form* of "cutting off from the people," or that capital punishment, shall be stoning. This law and the form of the penalty are both *new*.

Numbers xv., 37–41. The law requiring the wearing of "fringes on the borders of their garments" is *new*. This law, unlike the others, does not include "strangers," as it indicates race. There is nothing in either this law or the one before to indicate the time in which they were made; but their connection with the others raises a strong presumption that they were enacted at the same time, and *before* the repulse on "the hill even unto Hormah" and the rebellion of Korah.

Numbers xvi. contains an account of the rebellion of Korah and Dathan and Abiram and On,— the first a Levite, the other three Reubenites. That a second rebellion should have sprung up just at this time among the chief men, since Moses and Aaron had failed to take them into the promised land and were about to lead them back into the desert, is very credible. They gave as a justification for their rebellion the very plausible, not to say satisfactory, reason that Moses and Aaron had taken too much upon themselves, as the recent great reverses and the sufferings of the great and terrible wilderness journeyings threatened showed. Reuben was the eldest son, and Judah the fourth : why should not the children of Reuben lead in the march, and command instead of being placed behind Judah, as second in rank? Korah was a descendant of an *elder* son of Kohath than Elzaphan, who had been made " chief of the families of the Kohathites," and was cousin of Moses and Aaron, and might well aspire, after such disasters and such prospects, to a higher place. The time and circumstances correspond with the insurrection, and are its insufficient reason. The rebellion was nipped in the bud by the destruction of the leaders in a marvellous manner, and the right of Aaron to be the head of the priesthood is vindicated by the budding of his rod when all the other rods of the tribes budded not (chap. xvii.). Then follows, in chapter xviii., a repetition of many of the laws respecting the priesthood, with additions and changes, and a special charge to Aaron respecting his official duties and perquisites as distinguished from the Levites. These laws settled the questions in dispute between the Kohathites and the priests, Aaron and his sons. In verse 8, the "anointing" of the priests is spoken of, referring to the law which is recorded in Leviticus viii., 30. It is announced (chap. xviii., 12, 13) that the "first-fruits" should be given to Aaron, which is new; verse 14, every devoted thing is given to Aaron (Leviticus xxvii., 28), also new; verse 13, redeemed firstlings are to be Aaron's (Exodus xxxiv., 9), new.

Chapter xviii., 20, informs us that Aaron (the priesthood) should "have no inheritance in the land" as the Levites did, which is *new;* but the Levites must give a tenth part of their tithe to the priesthood (verses 26, 28). In this manner, all future dispute about the income of the priests is avoided. That this special legislation should have taken place at this critical time is strong evidence of the substantial accuracy of the history. And the legislation without the history would be strong evidence that something very important had transpired in the camp to render it necessary.

The nineteenth chapter contains a minute account of the preparation and use of the water of purification for any one who had been made unclean by contact with a dead body; the water to be used with the ashes of a red heifer. The *occasion* of this law is found in the plague, recorded in the sixteenth chapter, which carried off many thousands of the people. The whole ceremony was a most vigorous and efficient health law, and being enacted at this particular time corroborates the history.

All these laws indicate *special causes* for their enactment, and justify the belief that these chapters (xv. – xix.) were written at the time the people were encamped near Kadesh,— the xv., before their repulse, when they were soon expecting to enter the promised land, and the xvi.–xix., after that repulse. For farther evidence of the truth of these accounts, the reader is referred to *Undesigned Coincidences*, where the subject of Korah's rebellion is more fully examined.

V. After the wanderings in the wilderness were over and the people were encamped near Jordan, we find Moses giving more directions to the people, some entirely new, some modifications of previous laws. Let us see if there is anything in these directions or laws which will throw light upon the time and cause of their enactment, or anything in the condition of the people which will account for these laws being given at this particular time.

In Numbers xxviii., 1–8, the daily offering is spoken of, required in Exodus xxix., 38–42; and there is added to the original law the following amendment: "In the holy place shalt thou cause the strong wine to be poured." Both the place and the kind of wine are new. The original word for wine is translated in Leviticus x., 9, "strong drink." If it means "old wine," as the rabbins say, it implies that they were soon to be settled where they could keep wine till it was old, which they had not been able to do before. And the command to pour it "in the holy place" indicates that they might be tempted when settled in the land, by remoteness, to pour it elsewhere. Numbers xxviii., 4, and Exodus xxix., 39, are in the same words, showing that the writer of Numbers was familiar with the old law.

Numbers xxxviii., 9, 10. The Sabbath-day offering of

two lambs is new, and implies that they would be so situated that their flocks would permit such a draft on them, and also distinguish that day from other days.

Numbers xxix., 11-15. These new-moon offerings are *new*, and also imply an increase of their herds and flocks and vintage and olive-trees and grain, to justify another festival of their own nation at the time of the idolatrous festival of other nations, and thus secure them from joining their neighbors in idolatrous rites.

In chapter xxviii., 16-25, the proper manner of keeping the passover is described. In Leviticus xxiii., 5-8, no particulars are given. Verses 19-23 in Numbers are new. The animals, bullocks, and lambs to be offered in sacrifice on each of the seven days are *specified:* fourteen bullocks, forty-nine lambs, and seven goats in all. This free use of animals certainly indicates a larger supply at hand than they had previously had.

Numbers xxviii., 26-31. The description of "the day of first-fruits" differs in no important particular from that in Leviticus xxiii., 19-21. There is no obvious reason why it should have been inserted here, except that it was intimately connected with the new moon and passover.

Numbers xxix., 1-6, prescribes the sacrifices which are to be offered at the feast of trumpets, which is not done in Leviticus xxiii., 24, 25. This again shows clearly that flocks and herds would be more numerous, as they certainly would be as soon as they had settled in the promised land.

Numbers xxix., 7-11, describes the services of the holy convocation on the great day of atonement, and prescribes the sacrifices which must be offered, of which nothing is said in Leviticus xxiii., 26-32.

Numbers xxix., 12-34. The holy convocation of the feast of tabernacles and the feast itself are *fully* described *day by day;* but in Leviticus xxxiii., 34-44, only briefly. Numbers prescribes the sacrifices for each day, but says nothing about booths. Leviticus speaks of the booths, but does not specify the sacrifices or special ceremonies. The animals ordered for sacrifice during this greatest of festivals are seventy-one bullocks, fifteen rams, ninety-nine lambs, and seven goats. This number of animals indicates a near approach to more prosperous conditions than they were enjoying.

Numbers xxix., 35-40. We read in this section of the "solemn assembly" on the eighth day of the feast of the tabernacles, which is barely alluded to in Leviticus xxiii., 36. This shows clearly that this great feast, as well as the others, was not only rarely kept, but that they must have been destitute, when kept, of what gave them their hold upon the people in the land of promise. Nor is it probable that when they were settled in the promised land they were able to keep these great festivals, or did keep them, according to the ideal as prescribed in these laws. They all imply an *immediate* possession of their inheritance. And this necessary implication of the laws in themselves accords with the history and authenticates it.

Numbers xxx. It is evident from this chapter that the judges had had serious perplexity in administering the law of vows as recorded in the twenty-seventh chapter of Leviticus; and some general principles to aid the judges are laid down in this chapter. (1) Every man must do according to all that proceedeth out of his mouth; but (2) if a woman vowed, there were conditions of fulfilment depending on her father's hearing her; if (3) she was married or betrothed, there were conditions of fulfilment depending upon her husband or betrothed hearing her; if (4) she was a widow or divorced, all shall stand; if (5) she is a wife in her husband's house, the conditions of fulfilment will vary as he did or did not hear her vow.

There is nothing in this chapter to indicate when it was written; but as vows were often, if not always connected with sacrifices, it is very probable that the full treatment of that subject in connection with these great feasts may have opened this question of the obligation of vows, especially when the vow must be paid by the husband or guardian of the person making the vow.

Taking all these *new* laws and *amendments* of old laws into the account, it is quite impossible to escape the conclusion that they were written when the history affirms that they were written, and when the contents of the laws themselves require them to have been written. This origin of these laws, or the most skilful and criminal forgery, is the only possible conclusion of the whole matter.

SECTION III. UNDESIGNED COINCIDENCES.

I wish now to call attention to another class of phenomena denoting the time in which the Pentateuch was composed. I refer to *Undesigned Coincidences,*—correspondences so slight yet so peculiar as to show that an eye-witness recorded the events to which they relate.*

---

* About thirty years ago, I read a small work by Blunt on this subject. As all my references to that work are lost, I am unable to tell for how many of these coincidences I am indebted to him, and can make only this general acknowledgment.

(1) An instance of this kind is the rate of travelling attributed to the people on their departure from Egypt. In about six or eight days, we find that they had marched as far as Marah, which was two-thirds of the way to Mt. Sinai from Rameses. But they did not reach Sinai under forty-five days. What more natural than that they should travel thus rapidly the first part of the way to escape the enemy, and then slacken their speed to give repose to the feeble and time for the stragglers to come up? Besides, it will be found upon examination that they fled much more rapidly from Rameses till the passage of the Red Sea than they did afterwards. This is entirely natural; and, when we reflect that the writer has only incidentally given us a clew to discover that such was the fact, it forces on us the conviction that he was one of the company.*

(2) The original direction respecting the order of marching was changed for the greater convenience of those who bore the tabernacle and its furniture. It is distinctly stated in the general orders, as recorded in Numbers ii., that after *six* tribes have moved forward,

---

* The peculiar and apparently unreasonable route which Moses took in leaving Egypt, leading the people into a *cul de sac*,—the sea on the one hand and the mountains on the other, and Pharaoh behind them,— is attributed by the pious historian, writing perhaps half a century afterward, to the special direction of Jehovah to Moses in order probably that He might show forth His power to the fleeing nation, and give them courage to persist in the great undertaking of escaping from bondage and returning to the land of their remote ancestors. This may be so. But I am inclined to another, and to me more probable as it is a more reasonable, explanation of this remarkable mistake of Moses, as it appears to us without the historian's theory or knowledge of its cause. Let the reader bear in mind that God is spoken of by this very pious writer as directing everything and causing everything, and that Moses is scarcely a free agent in anything. Now, I submit as most probable that, when Pharaoh learned that the people had fled, he changed his mind and determined to intercept their march. He accordingly pursued with his horsemen and chariots, and succeeded in outflanking them and

when they decamp, then the Levites shall set forward with the tabernacle. But in the tenth chapter, where we have an account of their setting out on their march, we read that, after *three* tribes had set forward, the tabernacle was taken down, and the sons of Gershon and the sons of Merari set forward bearing the tabernacle. Then came three tribes more, and then the Kohathites set forward bearing the sanctuary, the holy utensils, the altars, and the ark. And a good reason appears why this change was made. The tabernacle would be set up ready to receive the sacred things as soon as those who bore them should arrive upon the ground of re-encampment.

(3) In the *fourth* chapter, we read that a division was made of the different parts of the tabernacle between the sons of Gershon, Merari, and Kohath. The sons of Gershon were to bear the coverings of the tabernacle; the sons of Merari were to bear the pillars and boards and sockets; the sons of Kohath were to bear the sacred vessels, the altars, and the ark. Now, if we turn to the *seventh* chapter, we read of the trains and

getting in their front before they had reached the north-western point of the sea. Moses had his choice either to fight Pharaoh, now in front of him, or flee as well as he could down the country by the side of the sea. He chose the latter alternative, and by removing his marching signal to the rear, and deceiving Pharaoh as to his true position, he gained time, by taking advantage of the darkness and of a very low stage of the water, to get the people over to the other side. When the day dawned, Pharaoh attempted to cross after them, but the muddy bottom and the return of deep water prevented him, and a large number of his army perished in the attempt. Moses turned down by the sea because he was compelled to by the position of the Egyptians; and after their wonderful escape the people saw in it the guidance of their God; and the devout historian of another generation introduces Jehovah as the counsellor and guide of Moses in the whole transaction. Nothing could be more natural. But the reader of today must recognize in his study of these early records this pervading language of piety, and interpret them accordingly. I am not satisfied with Brugsch's hypothesis respecting the route of the escaping Israelites.

wagons which were provided some days after to carry the tabernacle. Without giving the reason for the unequal distribution, *two wagons and four oxen* were given to the sons of Gershon, and *four wagons and eight oxen* to the sons of Merari. This difference in capacity for carrying freight corresponds to the difference in the materials which the two parties were to carry, Merari having much the heavier portion, as is found by looking back four chapters, where the distribution of materials is made. It is hardly credible that a later historian would have separated these items in this way, and yet have, thus incidentally, preserved the correspondence between the parts.

(4) The omission of the mention of Simeon in the blessings which Moses pronounced upon the tribes, as recorded in Deuteronomy xxxiii., has given rise to no little speculation. If we turn back to the twenty-fifth chapter of Numbers, a reason will be found for this omission which is entirely satisfactory. We read in the chapter referred to that a terrible plague smote the camp of Israel on account of the introduction of a Midianitish woman into the camp under very offensive circumstances. Twenty thousand died of the plague before it was stayed. This terrible calamity, which happened but a short time before Moses pronounced his blessings on the tribes, was caused by the act of "Zimri, the son of Salu, *a prince of the chief house of the Simeonites.*" It appears also that the plague was confined to the tribe of Simeon; for we find in the census, taken but a short time after, that this tribe had diminished thirty-seven thousand. It is not at all wonderful, therefore, that Moses should omit to bless such a tribe, when

their diminished numbers were a standing witness of God's displeasure, and when the plague, which had so devastated their part of the camp, had but just been stayed, and was fresh in the memory of all. Nor is this the conclusion of the matter. We find that, when the tribe took possession of the promised land, Simeon was made a barrier both of Egypt and the Philistines, so that he must first suffer in case of attack from that quarter. These facts, so purely incidental in the manner of their relation, scattered through different chapters, so perfectly accounting for other facts, remarkable in their character yet equally incidentally related, without any reasons given for such strange phenomena, bear with no little weight in the scale of the authenticity and age of these books. That they were not introduced into the Pentateuch for the purpose of supplying the material for this argument to future investigators of the age of the work is evident enough. The supposition is absurd.

(5) The account of the visit of Balaam for the purpose of cursing Israel demands notice. After the ineffectual attempts made by Balak, King of Moab, to induce Balaam to curse Israel, and after Balaam had obtained all the gifts which he was able to wring from the frightened king, we read, Numbers xxiv., 25, that "Balaam rose up and went and returned to his place." "His place," we find in chapter xxii., 5, to be "Pethor," a city of Mesopotamia, on the Euphrates. But we are surprised when we read in chapter xxxi., 8, where the chiefs of Midian are named who had been slain in battle, to find that "Balaam also, the son of Beor," was slain by the sword. How came he here, among the

Midianites? He had left Balak, King of Moab, "to return home." If we turn back to the twenty-second chapter, we find that the "elders of Midian" went with the elders of Moab, with the "rewards of divination in their hand," to invite Balaam to come and "curse Israel." The elders of Midian are no more mentioned in the history; yet in this brief line we find the cause of Balaam's taking Midian in his way, on his return home. More gifts he would obtain, if possible, before he left the country. He was killed while he stopped among that people to finish the object for which he had made his journey from the East. The presence of the historian of these facts on the spot where they transpired seems certain.

(6) In the account of the rebellion and destruction of Korah and his company there are some very striking indications of the writer's presence at the time. The leaders of the rebels, as we learn from Numbers xvi., 1, were "Korah, the son of Izhar, the son of Kohath, the son of Levi; and Dathan and Abiram, the sons of Eliab; and On, the son of Peleth, sons of *Reuben*." How came it to pass that the tribe of *Reuben*, or a part of it, and the Kohathites should be engaged in this rebellion? If we look back *thirteen chapters* to chapter iii., 29, we shall find that in recording the location of the Levites in the camp, the writer states that "the families of the sons of Kohath shall pitch on the side of the tabernacle *southward*." And still *further back*, in chapter ii., 10, we read that "on the *south side* shall be the standard of the camp of Reuben." At the distance of thirteen chapters, and separated from each other by one chapter, we find statements showing that

the tribe of Reuben and the Kohathites were on the same side of the camp, and in close proximity. It would be very easy for them, therefore, to confer together as they are represented as doing.

(7) Again, as we read the account of the punishment inflicted on the rebels, as recorded in the sixteenth chapter, we seem to see the earth open, and Korah, Dathan, and Abiram, and "their sons and their wives and their little children," all swallowed up alive. What, then, is our surprise, when we read, *ten chapters later*, in the twenty-sixth chapter, which contains a record of events which transpired *thirty-six years afterwards*, that "the children of Korah died not." We turn back to re-examine the sixteenth chapter, to see if we were mistaken. We there find that the people are commanded to "depart from the tents of those wicked men." "So they gat up from the tabernacle of Korah, Dathan, and Abiram, on every side." This tabernacle appears to have been occupied in common by the rebels as their place of meeting with their associates. And then we read that "Dathan and Abiram came out and stood in the door of their tents, and their wives and their sons and their little ones." This public tent of meeting, it seems, stood near the tents of these two men, who were Reubenites, and not near the tent of Korah, who was a Levite; so that when "the earth opened her mouth and swallowed them up, and their houses [tents] and all the men [that is, the rebels] that appertained to Korah, and all their goods," the children of Korah, who were in the family tent among the Levites, were not destroyed. Thus the apparent contradiction is reconciled in such a manner as to indicate that an eye-wit-

ness was the historian. I cannot forbear recalling the attention of the reader to another feature of this transaction. Korah, the leader of this rebellion, was son of Izhar, the *second* son of Kohath, Amram, the father of Moses and Aaron, being the first. But the *chief* of the Kohathites was Elzaphan, the son of Uzziel, the *fourth* son of Kohath. It was natural, therefore, that envious feelings should arise, on his part, against the hardship of the younger branch of the family. The posterity of Reuben, the *eldest son* of Jacob, would likewise be not a little dissatisfied that Judah, a younger brother, should be placed at the head of all the tribes.

(8) In the tenth chapter of Leviticus, we read that "Nadab and Abihu, the sons of Aaron, took either of them his censer, and put fire therein, and put incense thereon, and offered *strange fire* before the Lord." For this act, they were smitten dead by fire "from the Lord." And "Mishael and Elzaphan, the sons of Uzziel, the uncle of Aaron," carried their dead bodies "from before the sanctuary out of the camp." No cause for this high-handed act of these two sons of Aaron is given by the writer; but he immediately after records a new law: "Do not *drink wine nor strong drink*, thou [Aaron] nor thy sons with thee, when ye go into the tabernacle of the congregation, *lest ye die*. . . . And that ye may put a difference between holy and unholy, and between clean and unclean." The cause of this new enactment was, most obviously, the sacrilegious act of Aaron's sons, committed when they were intoxicated, and did not put a difference between "holy and unholy, and between clean and unclean." Such gross outrages must not be repeated, and a law is enacted to prevent their recur-

rence. Here we not only have a new law to meet an emergency, but we also have a law based upon the probable condition of those two priests, when the fact of their being intoxicated is not mentioned.

(9) A farther coincidence demands notice in this connection. This act of Nadab and Abihu took place on the eighth day after the tabernacle was erected; for in Exodus xl., 2, we read that the "tabernacle of the tent of the congregation" was to be set up on "the first day of the first month." In the thirteenth verse, we read that Aaron and his sons were to be anointed and clothed in their holy garments for their sacred office. After *seven* chapters in Leviticus, giving directions about particular sacrifices which were to be offered in the tabernacle, we find in the eighth and ninth chapters a specific account of the consecration of Aaron and his sons which continued seven days (chap. viii., 33). On the eighth day (chap. ix., 1), new ceremonies were performed by these priests, their seven days of confinement and seclusion being over; and it is on this eighth day that these sons of Aaron, once more associating with their friends, indulged probably so freely in the use of the cup as to profane the Lord by attempting to serve in their holy office while intoxicated. How natural that men who had been accustomed to the moderate social glass should indulge thus freely after such a week of seclusion! Yet of all this series of causes the writer says not a word; nor is there the remotest ground for the supposition that he had arranged these incidents to furnish us with this argument for the age of his writing. That the narrator was on the spot and related what he saw is too obvious to require comment.

(10) Nor have we yet done with this account. These dead bodies were carried "out of the camp" just *six* days before the passover. Turning forward now *twenty-five* chapters, which are filled with the transactions of these six days, to the ninth chapter of Numbers, we come to the fourteenth day of the first month, on which the passover was to be kept. We here find an account of its observance; and we read "there were *certain men who were defiled by the dead body of a man*, so that they could not keep the passover on that day; and they came before Moses and Aaron," and said that they were defiled and were thus prevented from offering their offering unto the Lord. "Seven days," which were necessary for the purification of those who were unclean by contact with a dead body, had not transpired since Mishael and Elzaphan had carried out their kinsmen's dead bodies, and hence they could not eat of the passover or offer the sacrifice. It is probable that these were the men who came to Moses, as above related; for such a complaint would be likely to originate in the first instance among the chief men, and these men were of that class. The phrase, "the dead body of a man," being the legal term by which ritual uncleanness from contact with the dead is expressed, by no means shows, or implies, that there was but *one* dead body. Three implied conditions are found in this narration, two of them connected with other facts related ten and twenty chapters distant, and *so* related as to show clearly that the writer of these accounts must have been an eye-witness of what he relates, or at least a contemporary of the events, and narrating what he well knew was transpiring. Let

these ten illustrations of "undesigned coincidences" suffice.

SECTION IV.   EVIDENCE FROM MINUTENESS OF DETAILS.

Another characteristic of these books, showing their journal-like character, and indicating a writer in the camp of Israel, is found in the *minuteness of the details* in many parts of the narrative, and their repetition under such circumstances as to exculpate any later writer from being the author of such useless definiteness and wearisome repetitions; and yet these same circumstances demanded of the desert-journalist just such a minuteness and repetition. These phenomena have a twofold power: they equally *demand* an ancient, and *forbid* a modern, writer. Let us now examine some of them.

(1) In the census of the people, an account of which is contained in the first chapter of Numbers, there is an illustration of the recording, at the time, of work done, or of the journal-like character of the book. First, we have the names, not only of the superintendents of the census of each tribe, but also the names of their fathers, which it is not probable would have been given by a writer in the time of Ezra. Then we have repeated before the round number of each tribe the formula under which the census was taken, making a repetition of the same words twelve times, which it is difficult to believe an historian a thousand or eight hundred years later would have done; but it is very probable it would be done, when the separate papers of enrolment were passed in and recorded or filed. Seven lines of the nine which constituted the return of each tribe are,

word for word, the same. A later historian of the transaction, with these returns before him, would, at the most, have written the heading but once; and then, after this description of the persons enrolled, he would have named the tribes and their number in order. Of all this, Josephus only says (chap. viii., 2), "The number of the offerers [of the half-shekels, as represented by this census] was six hundred and five thousand five hundred and fifty."

(2) Another illustration of the time and place of writing this Book of Numbers is contained in the second chapter, in which the order of the encampment is specified with great minuteness. The names of the tribes are given, and also the name of the "captain" of the tribe is given, and, yet more, the name of the captain's father, and also the number in the tribe according to the census, and, finally, the whole number in each of the four divisions which were encamped on the four sides of the tabernacle, the account filling thirty-two verses of the chapter. All this would be very necessary in the order for arranging the camp at first; but what historian in the time of Ezra would have given an account of the camp in this manner? Josephus illustrates this admirably (chap. xii., 5): "When they set up the tabernacle, they received it into the midst of their camp, three of the tribes pitching their tents on each side of it." And all that is said by Josephus respecting the elaborate arrangement in the next chapter — abridged in the paragraph below — is that "the priests had the first place about the tabernacle; then the Levites."

(3) Then, in the third chapter, there is a record of the distribution of the material of the tabernacle and

its furniture among the priests and Levites, whose order of encampment is minutely specified inside the other tribes and around the tabernacle, which was their special charge. The sons of Gershon shall have charge "of the covering of the tent and the hanging for the door of the tabernacle of the congregation and the hangings of the court and the curtain for the door of the court . . . and the cords of it." And the charge of Kohath "shall be the ark and the table and the candlestick and the altars and the vessels of the sanctuary and the hanging and all the service thereof." "And the charge of the sons of Merari shall be the boards of the tabernacle, and the bars thereof, and the pillars thereof, and the sockets thereof, and all the vessels thereof, . . . and the pillars of the court round about, and their sockets and their pins and their cords." This has certainly the air of the camp and the desert and the time of the great migration.

(4) But there is yet more of this, and more even, if possible, to the purpose. How shall that portion of the tabernacle furniture which the sons of Kohath are to carry, and which was holy, and which none but a priest could handle on pain of death, be approached, prepared, and borne? In the fourth chapter, from the fourth to the tenth verses, we have a minute description of the manner in which Aaron and his sons "shall cover the ark of testimony with the covering veil, and shall put thereon the covering of badgers' skins, and shall spread over it a cloth wholly of blue, and shall put in the staves thereof," by which it is to be carried. "And upon the table of shew bread they shall spread a cloth of blue and put thereon the dishes, and the spoons, and

the bowls and covers, ... and they shall spread upon them a cloth of scarlet, and cover the same with a covering of badgers' skins, and shall put in the staves thereof." And the "candlestick, and his lamps, and his tongs, and his snuff dishes, and all the oil vessels thereof," are to be covered with "a cloth of blue," and to be put into "a covering of badgers' skins and put upon a bar"; "and upon the golden altar they shall spread a cloth of blue and cover it with a covering of badgers' skins," "and they shall take all the instruments of ministry ... and put them in a cloth of blue, and cover them with a covering of badgers' skins, and shall put them on a bar; and they shall take away the ashes from the altar, and spread a purple cloth thereon; and they shall put upon it all the vessels thereof, wherewith they minister about it, even the censers, the flesh-hooks and the shovels and the basins, all the vessels of the altar, and they shall spread over it a covering of badgers' skins, and put to the staves of it"; then, and not till then, the sons of Kohath shall come to bear them. Then the service of the sons of Gershon and Merari is to be arranged by Aaron and his sons, and a census of these families is to be taken of all males from thirty to fifty years old, that proper relays and reliefs might be made while marching and in camp.

What I affirm is that all this minute direction and organization of the Levites and priests indicates, *demands* for its justification, its cause, the precise time, and place, and circumstances which the history describes; and that no historian of the nation in the time of Ezra and Nehemiah would have written in this manner. I pass by the fact that the "shittim wood," of which the wood-work of the tabernacle and its furniture was made, was abundant about Mount Sinai and rare in Canaan, and that the "badgers' skins" were most probably the skins of a fish which abounded in the Red Sea, as I do not wish to introduce anything as fact into this Study which may be challenged.

(5) But I have not done. I must challenge the reader's patience still further. I cite as a striking proof of the authenticity and age of the Pentateuch the minute account of the offerings made by the princes of Israel to the tabernacle during the period of its dedication. It is contained in the seventh chapter of Numbers, commencing with the twelfth verse. Each prince brought his offering on a day by himself, so that on twelve different days we have the entry made by the scribe in the journal of the offering. Each prince offered the same gifts. The wording of the entry is in each case the same. Leave a blank in either of the entries for the names of the princes, and they will read alike. I will give the first entry: "And he that offered his offering the first day was Nahshon, the son of Amminadab, of the tribe of Judah; and his offering was one silver charger, the weight thereof was a hundred and thirty shekels, one silver bowl of seventy shekels, after the shekel of the sanctuary; both of them were full of fine flour mingled with oil for a meat-offering; one spoon of ten shekels of gold full of incense; one young bullock, one ram, one lamb of the first year, for a burnt-offering; one kid of the goats for a sin-offering; and for a sacrifice of peace-offerings, two oxen, five rams, five he-goats, five lambs of the first year. This was the offering of Nahshon, the son of Amminadab."

Now, instead of simply saying that each of the other princes of the tribes offered in like manner the same offerings unto the Lord, the writer goes on and repeats this inventory eleven times, through eighty verses. It is incredible that a later writer, giving such an account, should proceed in this manner. It appears altogether like an entry made by the scribe to see that the tribes did what was required of them, though no mention of such requisition is made in the record. I have had the curiosity to turn again to Josephus to see how, in his summary of the law, he manages this matter, and will quote the passage which relates to these offerings, that the reader may see the difference between the style of a later writer and that of the old journalists. Josephus says: "Every head of a tribe brought a bowl, a charger, and a spoon of ten daricks full of incense. Now the charger and bowl were of silver, and together they weighed two hundred shekels, but the bowl cost no more than seventy shekels; and these were full of fine flour mingled with oil, such as they used on the altar about the sacrifices. They brought also a young bullock and a ram, with a lamb a year old, for a whole burnt-offering; as also a goat, for the forgiveness of sins. Every one of the heads of the tribes brought also other sacrifices, called peace-offerings; for every day, two bulls and five rams, with lambs of a year old and kids of the goats. These heads of the tribes were twelve days in sacrificing, one sacrificing every day." The contrast between these two accounts clearly shows us how an historian living long after the events, as in the time of Ezra, would have managed such a subject.

(6) Another illustration of this head of my argument is found in the wearisomely minute diagnostics of the leprosy in men, houses, and garments (Leviticus xiii., xiv.). Two long chapters, of nearly sixty verses each, are filled with the repulsive details of the indications and purification of this most loathsome of all diseases. I must be excused from quoting any of it. No more modern historian would thus burden his pages; but then and there it was necessary, for definite rules must be given for the guidance of the priests. Indeed, the whole of this portion of the Pentateuch which refers to ritual impurities indicates clearly enough that it had its birth in the camp, among a people just emerging from barbarism.

(7) Perhaps the most marked of all these laboriously minute descriptions and repetitions is to be found in the last half of Exodus, where the tabernacle and its furniture and the priests' garments are described in the most accurate manner, even to the tassels and pins and taches (Exodus xxv. – xxx.). Moses brings this minute description of the whole sacerdotal dress and tabernacle construction and incense manufacture with him from the Mount. It is precisely like the specifications in a modern contract for building a dwelling-house or making a garment or a confection, but more minute, if possible. The work is given out by Moses; and, as the workmen bring back to him the portion which they undertook to make, it is entered again with the same minute description in the Pentateuch (Exodus xxxvi. – xxxix.). So that we have a duplicate description of all these articles, so wearisomely minute that we

can hardly have patience to read it once. Admit that this was written on the spot, and all this minuteness and duplication is accounted for: deny this, and there is no possible reason why such a minute detail of these articles should be repeated, even if we can discover why they should be once described. It seems incredible that any later writer could have done it. Of the "pattern given in the Mount," which is so minutely described, before the work was done, in the Pentateuch, Josephus only says (chap. v., 8), " He [God] had suggested to him [Moses] that he would have a tabernacle built for him, and that the tabernacle should be of such measure and construction as he had showed him." Josephus then gives a careful description of the work. There is no repetition of particulars.

To feel the full force of this argument, it is necessary that one should read carefully the account in the Pentateuch, and at one sitting, if possible.

I should be glad to go into a consideration of the specific directions given touching many of the conditions of camp life, and especially those health regulations which it was necessary for a people thus sojourning to observe, and which no modern historian could dwell upon so long and minutely as they are dwelt upon in the Pentateuch; but the nature of the subjects, as well as the great length of my Study, requires that I should pass them over. Their bearing upon the point which I am considering is clear and strong; and, in connection with some of the circumstances which I have already referred to, they furnish evidence, almost conclusive in itself, of the antiquity of the work in which they are contained.

SECTION V. EVIDENCE FROM CHASMS IN THE HISTORY.

The *chasms* in the history are another indication of the antiquity of the Pentateuch. (1) The space of nearly four hundred years, according to the reckoning which commends itself to many scholars, from the descent of Jacob and his family into Egypt to the departure of the people, is passed over in almost entire silence; and so also are the youth and manhood of Moses, in which Josephus and the rabbins revel and glory. Only those incidents are mentioned which are necessary to an introduction to the great work of deliverance from Egyptian bondage. We can hardly suppose that a writer of the time of Ezra would have left such gaps in his history. The particular and wonderful events in the life of Moses before his flight to Midian, which tradition had handed down, and which attracted the Jews in the time of Josephus, could hardly have escaped the notice of earlier writers. They would have filled up these chasms with such traditions as had come down to them respecting the marvellous life of their great law-giver. That such would have been their course can hardly be doubted by any one who is acquainted with Jewish writers, and knows how prone they were to introduce traditionary tales where historical facts failed them.

Nor is the chasm referred to, all. Thirty-seven years, covering a large portion of the period of the wandering in the wilderness, is left an entire blank, and we know almost nothing of what transpired, except the stations which from time to time the people occupied. A more attractive field for the growth of traditions could not be imagined; and not to enter it would require more regard for historical truth, or a nicer discrimination between what is true and what is false, than later writers of that nation have shown in their works, or than some modern critics give them credit for. I cannot introduce illustrations to show the correctness of these remarks. Those readers who are familiar with Jewish literature do not need them, and those who are not will find enough of them in the writings of Philo, Josephus, the Talmudists, and the rest. Admit that the principal parts of the last four books of the Pentateuch are the work of a writer, a scribe or scribes, contemporary with the events which are recorded in them, and these chasms are easily accounted for: assume any later period for their composition, and they present insurmountable obstacles.

SECTION VI. EVIDENCE FROM EGYPTIAN CUSTOMS.

I should be glad to go at length into a consideration of the minute and circumstantial references which we find in the Pentateuch to Egyptian customs. But I must confine myself to one, as an illustration of many, which impresses deeply upon the mind the opinion that an eye-witness must have recorded them. A resident in Egypt, and none other, could thus have colored the history with such delicate touches denoting his age and residence. In the fifth chapter of Exodus, the historian gives an account of the additional labor which was put upon the Hebrews when they complained of their tasks, and asked leave to go into the country for three days to worship. "I will not give you straw," said Pharaoh. "Go ye, get you straw where ye can find it. ... So the people were scattered abroad throughout all the land of Egypt to gather *stubble* instead of *straw*." The "straw" was that which had been broken upon the threshing-floor; the "stubble" was what had been left standing in the field after reaping. If we turn now to Wilkinson's *Manners and Customs of the Ancient Egyptians* (Vol. VI., page 86), we shall find an engraving, taken from the ancient tombs, in which is represented the gathering of wheat. The reapers are represented as cutting off only the heads of the grain, which they put in baskets, and leaving the "stubble" nearly as high as their shoulders behind them. This was the "stubble" which the Hebrews went out to gather, not the short stubble which was left when the straw was cut near the ground. The overtasked Hebrews had not the privilege of going to the threshing-floors and getting their "straw": they were compelled to gather this high "stubble" in the field. In the same work, we find illustrations of brick-making, and bricks made with straw are found in the ruins of the ancient cities.

Such minute knowledge of the manners of Egypt as the writer of the Pentateuch everywhere shows, and which it would cover pages to describe, confirms the opinion of its Mosaic origin. It is hardly conceivable that a later writer could have so fully informed himself of ancient customs as to have spoken of them so incidentally and yet so accurately and minutely.

SECTION VII. EVIDENCE FROM EGYPTIAN WORDS AND RITES.

Another evidence of the early origin of the Pentateuch is found in the use of Egyptian words, the adoption of Egyptian customs in their worship, both in utensils, altars, and robes, and also in the establishment of a priesthood and ritual. In the first sixteen chapters of Exodus, in which the bondage and escape of the people are described, no less than forty-eight words, exclusive of proper names, of Egyptian origin, are used, if such scholars as Gesenius and Bunsen can be relied upon, to say nothing of Seyffarth and Harkavy and Wilkinson. Egypt must have been the native land of the author. He is familiar with the manners and customs of the people. The whole account is evidence of such an author. The Urim and Thummim were Egyptian symbols of Truth and Justice, and were worn by the judge or priest in the breastplate which was over his priestly dress, as is shown in Wilkinson's *Ancient Egyptians*. The dress of the priests is not unlike that of the Egyptian priests — linen — as represented in the same work. Their bathing and shaving the whole body were the same also. Even the ark of the covenant and the cherubim over it are copied from those used in Egypt, as may be seen in Wilkinson, Vol. V., page 276. As far as modern studies in Egyptian archæology have gone, they confirm the accuracy of the description of the manners, laws, and language of that ancient people made by the writer of the Pentateuch, and remand its composition to an early age and a native of the country.

It has been objected to the antiquity and unity of the Pentateuch that such a complicated ritual and comprehensive body of laws could not have sprung into existence at once; that generations, centuries, were necessary to evolve and mature them. It is forgotten by those who present this objection that the Egyptians were an old nation when Jacob's family went among them. They had the most attractive and elaborate ritual the world knew,— priests, temples, altars, sacrifices, were almost everywhere. Their laws were the mature wisdom of ages. How easy was it, comparatively speaking, for the law-giver of Israel to arrange, with the aid of such a ritual and such laws, the ritual and laws which we find in the Pentateuch, so similar to those of Egypt as to reveal their relationship, and so dissimilar as to prevent confounding them, and establishing the independence of their author! No careful student of the Hebrew code and ritual can fail to see the influence of an Egyptian education and residence upon the law-giver; so that the objection is itself transformed into an argument in favor of the antiquity of the Pentateuch and even of its Mosaic origin. He would naturally, trained as he had been, construct a full code and ritual for the recently delivered people. Nor is it any valid evidence, scarcely a presumption, that he did not do it, because they were but imperfectly administered, and in some respects apparently persistently violated for centuries. The code and the ritual sprang fully formed, mature, from the brain of Moses, like Minerva from the brain of Jupiter. The people were not able to understand or appreciate but a small part of them at first, and some portions of them were very probably found impracticable or so burdensome as to compel neglect. The code and the ritual were ideal, and could not in every particular be made real. The servile, emancipated race developed slowly up to the standard of their law whose requirements were ever before them. Their barbarism gradually wore off, and the knowledge of the one only God increased, and diminished their belief in other gods and their relish of idolatrous rites. The people *grew up* to the law, as Christians are growing up to Christianity. The gospel reads to-day as it did eighteen centuries ago, but how differently it is understood and practised! The Mosaic code and ritual read the same through all the tumultuous period of the Judges and the revolution under Samuel, and during the monarchy; but how differently were they regarded as the people sloughed off their barbarisms and improved in knowledge!

SECTION VIII. NO EVIDENCE OF ENACTMENTS AFTER THE TIME OF MOSES.

One point further, and I will close. The Pentateuch concludes its history with the death of Moses, and professes to contain only those laws and rites which were prescribed by him. *There is not a particle of reliable evidence, either external or internal, that a single law recorded in the Pentateuch was the work of the period subsequent to the time of Moses.* I affirm this with the emphasis of assurance. The possession of the promised land is always spoken of as future. New laws are given, new regulations are established on the banks of the Jordan, just before the people passed over to take possession of their country, such as their changed condition would require. No laws were made afterwards of which we have any record which were fundamental. All appeals are made to the law of Moses.

So much for the *antiquity* of the Pentateuch. Who was its writer? To answer this question is no purpose of this Study. Probably Moses was the principal author. I am aware that one objection which has weight in some minds is made to the Mosaic authorship of the Pentateuch: it is that he is spoken of in the third person in the historical portions. This is true; and admitting that it has weight so far as the Mosaic authorship is concerned, it has no weight whatever against my position; for I am not proving that Moses was the writer of the Pentateuch, but that it was chiefly at least composed during his life. Against this position, the objection has no force whatever. But I am by no means willing to give it the weight which is claimed for it as conclusive against the Mosaic authorship under any circumstances. Xenophon is admitted on all hands to have written the *Anabasis*, and yet he never speaks of himself in the first person, though he is the principal character in the work. Who can dogmatically assert that Moses did not do the same thing? Besides, who can say that Moses did not adopt the usual practice of early times, as indicated both in history and in monuments, of employing a scribe, or scribes, who took note of passing events, as well as writing out the laws, who would naturally speak of Moses in the third person?

The whole book has the style and coloring, the contents and structure, of a writing of the Mosaic age. A few passages of later date can easily be accounted for as *scholia* — explanatory clauses — which have been introduced into the text by later copyists and readers. Some apparent or real contradictions can be easily disposed of by the same method, or as failures in the memory of the original writer. As well might one challenge the antiquity of the pyramid because he had found a modern stone imbedded in one of its courses. Whether its condition could be accounted for or not, no antiquarian would think of pronouncing the monument of Cheops a work of the Ptolemies, standing in its hoary presence, with the voice of history sounding in his ears. As no astronomer would be accounted sane who should dispute that the sun is the source of light because a few dark spots are found on its surface, so no scholar who has surveyed all sides of this subject in the full light of modern discoveries can reasonably deny to the Mosaic age the production of the Pentateuch on account of alleged modern interpolations, imperfect genealogies, or contradictory dates and names which are found in it.

SECTION IX. RESULTS.

It results from the foregoing investigation : —

I. That that portion of the Hebrew Scriptures called the Pentateuch, or the Five Books of Moses, can be traced by a common name — "The Book of the Law," "The Law given by Moses," "The Law," and other titles — from the time of Christ back through all the extant literature of the nation — prose and poetry, prophecy and proverb, history and psalm — till the time of David, and in all fragments of its literature of an earlier date ; —

II. That all the passages quoted from the book with these titles are found in the Pentateuch, and often its peculiar phraseology is preserved in the quotation, showing that the book is proved to be the same by its contents as well as by its title ; —

III. That there is not the slightest hint in the historical books that these laws were enacted or revised in any later time than that of the Mosaic age; all Jewish opinions to this effect being of a much later date, and based upon no historical evidence whatever; —

IV. That the language of the Pentateuch, its peculiar phrases and "archaic words," shows that it must have been written some centuries before any other of the extant Hebrew writings, thus remitting its composition to several generations before the time of David, as the language of the earliest Psalms, which are free from them, witnesses; —

V. That the contents of the Pentateuch, the journal-like arrangement of its events and laws, the constant assumption or implication that it was written in a camp, and many of its laws adapted only to camp life, the amendments of laws when on the borders of the promised land to fit them to the changed condition and wants of the people, the inventories of gifts, and the record of specifications for wood-work, and curtains, and garments, and vessels for sacred use, the record of incidents which caused new laws to be enacted or old laws to be amended, the incidental and most obviously undesigned coincidences of events which are separated by many chapters and much time, confirm the previous historic and linguistic evidence of the early origin of the Pentateuch, and place its composition in the Mosaic age, and prove its direct or indirect Mosaic authorship; —

VI. That the tumultuous anarchical times before the accession of David to the throne render it very probable that sections of the law may have been misplaced, possibly lost; that some of the historical sections may have been disarranged; and that as time passed on old names were modernized, obscure incidents explained, and modern words and phrases sometimes substituted for the obsolete originals; but none of these modern explanations and interpolations and supposed corrections in the least degree affecting the force of the argument derived from the above-mentioned considerations of the age and at least the principal authorship of the work;—

VII. That, notwithstanding the difficulties attending the reference of this work to so early an age and authorship, they vanish into comparative unimportance when compared with those which attend any other theory of its composition, especially that which refers it to the time of Ezra, or accounts for it by miscellaneous aggregations made during the ten centuries which transpired between Moses and Nehemiah;—

VIII. And, finally, that the only reasonable, and indeed the necessary, inference to be drawn from these facts—the historical references to this book by the same names to the earliest times; the quotations made from it in later writings corresponding in minute particulars to passages found in it; the archaisms with which it abounds; the journal and camp-like arrangement and tone of its laws; the undesigned coincidences, indicating a writer on the spot; the occasional explanation of antique words, names, and customs; and the insuperable difficulties of fixing upon any other period for its composition—is that the Pentateuch belongs to the Mosaic age, and fixes the authorship of the book upon Moses and his contemporaries or immediate successors.

CONCLUSION.

DIFFICULTIES OF ANY THEORY OF UNBELIEF.

I KNOW the objections raised, the suspicion surmised, the prejudices appealed to; but I also know that there are difficulties in unbelief as well as in belief. It is often supposed that there are no difficulties trailing after denial; that some belief is not professed or implied when another is rejected. But he who denies the antiquity of the Pentateuch will be required by that denial to believe some things which will stagger reason and forbid faith. That very denial will compel him to adopt a positive opinion respecting the origin of the Pentateuch, which will draw after it difficulties more insolvable and facts more incredible than the plagues of Egypt or the refluent waves of the Red Sea. For he must believe that an unbroken chain of writers from the days of Josephus to the time of David, including philosophers, historians, poets, prophets, have quoted different books under the same title, and containing the same laws, expressed in the same words; that, between the translation of the Septuagint, in the golden reign of Philadelphus, and the time of the prophet Malachi, about a century, this "Book of the Law of Moses" was mostly written and palmed off upon the Jewish scribes as of Mosaic origin, and gravely translated by them into Greek at his command; or that, between the time of Malachi and the time of Ezra, about half a century more, some one or more of the returned exiles constructed a work which received the approbation of both prophets and rulers, people and priests, as the "Book of Moses" by whose laws their fathers had been guided; or that Ezra himself codified and published the national laws under the title of the "Laws of Moses," or invented nearly all of them, and succeeded in making the people receive them as such, either by gross fraud or because they were really of Mosaic origin, and yet his history makes *no mention* of such a wonderful work in narrating the invaluable services rendered to the people by this efficient ruler; or that, a century before, Hilkiah and Shaphan imposed a code under the name of "The Book of the Law of the Lord by Moses" upon King Josiah and all the nation, and that Hezekiah had no such "Book of the Law of Moses" as the historian affirms, and that Amaziah did not quote from it when he said, as it "is written in the Book of the Law of Moses," and that Jehoshaphat did not send out the scribes to teach that book when they "took the Book of the Law of the Lord with them," and that Jehoash had some other book under the name of "the Law" given him when he was anointed king, and that David did not refer to it when he charged Solomon to have regard to what "is written in the Law of Moses." He must believe, moreover, that different books and different codifications of the laws of the people from time to time are thus referred to, when not one lisp in the whole history or poetry or prophecy of the nation can be found to that effect. He must believe that the nation was so stupid as to permit it, and its historians so careless as not to mention it either to the honor or the disgrace of any scribe or king. He must believe that in the time of Ezra or Josiah a writer succeeded in imitating the ancient style of the Mosaic age so perfectly that all the scribes and priests were deceived into the belief that it was the work of Moses, even when there was no evidence that he ever wrote such a book, or that such a book had ever existed in the nation. Nay, more: he must believe that all its complicated and burdensome laws were received at once and adopted as the code of the nation, *because* they believed them to be of Mosaic origin, and submitted to the severe discipline which these laws imposed, without once questioning the authenticity of the book or the authority of the law-giver. He must believe that the writer not only invented the accounts of the building of the tabernacle, and wearisomely repeated them, and also introduced the repetitious descriptions of the offerings and the consecration of the sacred things, but he must believe that he could luckily hit upon or skilfully invent those numerous *undesigned coincidences* which are scattered all through the book, so evidently unobserved by the writer himself. He must believe that the writer — guilty of one of the grossest impositions ever practised upon a people — was never suspected, much less accused, of fraud, but that his spurious work was received and adopted without a word of complaint, suspicion, or hesitation by a whole nation. He must believe that no "Book of the Law" was in existence during the reign of David, and that all the historians, prophets, and poets which have referred to it in an unbroken series from his time down to the time of Nehemiah and Malachi, Sirach and Philo, were mistaken, or else he must believe that a gross corruption of the old copy was made, and made in so skilful a manner that no one detected it then, or can now tell with any certainty the new portions which were added to the old book. The learned men of Jehoshaphat, the scholarly priest and scribe of Josiah, the noble Ezra, the skilful Nehemiah, never suspected the fraud, never discovered the cheat. Nor did the prophets Joel and Hosea, Isaiah and Jeremiah, Haggai and Malachi, have a suspicion that "the Law," "the Laws of Moses," "the Law of the Lord," on which they based all their predictions, and to which they appealed in confirmation of all their threatenings and promises, was a mere collection made from age to age of the laws of the nation, and attributed, by a pious fraud or illiterate mistake, to their great deliverer, Moses, to give them sanctity and power over the people. Surely, a louder curse would have leaped from the fiery lips of Isaiah upon the head of such a deceiver than he ever uttered against the hypocritical priests who "trampled the courts of the Lord." Yet such must be his belief who disbelieves.

Adopting the canon of Hume, that of two miracles we should believe that which is the less marvellous and incredible, I accept the miracle, if it be one, of the Mosaic origin of the Pentateuch, rather than the theory which makes it either the growth of centuries or the work of a modern Jew of the time of Ezra. The difficulties attending the last theory are vastly greater than those which surround the first. As easily could I believe that the basaltic pillars which compose the Giant's Causeway were the work of the fabulous race whose name they bear, and not the production of the earth's central fires. I believe, then, that the Pentateuch is a work of the Mosaic age, and largely the work of Moses himself; that it has come down to us with few, very few, dislocations, interpolations, and corruptions; and that it will be handed down to coming ages as an admired monument of the wisdom, learning, and arts of that remote age,— as a monument of an early revelation of the divine will, to restore and elevate the race. I believe that the more thorough the investigations are which are directed to the examination of this book, the more profound and searching the scholarship which is devoted to the inquiry of its age and authorship, the more successful the endeavors of the explorers of the ancient monuments on the Nile and the Tigris in exhuming sculptured tablets and opening tombs whose walls are pictured history, the more brilliant the success of the Rawlinsons, the Layards, and the Hinckses, the Smiths and the Sayces, in deciphering the cuneiform inscriptions on the walls of the palaces of the successors of Ninus, and of the Wilkinsons and the Lepsiuses and the Mariettes in interpreting the painted symbols and hieroglyphic histories in the tombs of the Pharaohs contemporary with Abraham and Joseph and Moses, the more certainty will be given to the conclusions which I have reached, or, at least, to which I have pointed the way: that THE PENTATEUCH IS SUBSTANTIALLY OF THE MOSAIC AGE, AND LARGELY, EITHER DIRECTLY OR INDIRECTLY, OF MOSAIC AUTHORSHIP.

ANALYTICAL INDEX.

PAGE

INTRODUCTORY ON KUENEN'S "RELIGION OF ISRAEL."

Style of the Work, and Test of the Truth of Later Writers, ... 7–10
Illustrations of Perversions of History by Priests and Prophets, ... 11–13
Theory of Human Progress the Test of All History, . 14–16
Point of Departure in the Inquiry of the Historic Truth, and Dr. Kuenen's Method of Argument, . 16–24
Reform under Hezekiah and Josiah, ... 24–27
Hilkiah's "Book of the Law," 27–32
The Law the Work of Ezekiel and Ezra (Leviticus xviii., xxvi.), ... 33–36
Objection that "No Mention is made of any such Work as the Pentateuch in any Work written before the Captivity" examined, ... 37–58
Testimony of the Book of the Kings, ... 37–39
    "   "   "   "   Chronicles, ... 39–42
    "   "   "   "   Joshua, Judges, Samuel, 42–47
    "   "   "   "   Ezra, Nehemiah, . . 47–57
Conclusion 57
Appendix A: "The Bible for Learners." Some of its Theories noticed,— Sinai, Samson, Korah, . 59–65
Appendix B: Some of Dr. Kuenen's Theories examamined,— Priests, Levites, etc., ... 66–69
    No Prophetic Writing till Eighth Century, . 70
    Not One Psalm from David, ... 70
    Different Documents in Exodus and Numbers, ... 71

A STUDY OF THE PENTATEUCH.

	PAGE
INTRODUCTION,	75–81
EXTERNAL EVIDENCES,	82

I. *Christ to Malachi.*

1st Esdras,	83
1st Maccabees,	84
Ecclesiasticus,	84
Septuagint Version,	84
Samaritan Pentateuch,	84

II. *Malachi to Captivity.*

Malachi,	85
Haggai,	85
Zechariah,	85
Nehemiah,	85–86
Ezra,	86–87

III. *Captivity to David.*

(1) Historical Books, remarks on, . . . 87–90

Books of the Kings,	90–100
Josiah,	90–93
Hezekiah,	93–94
Amaziah,	94
Jehoash,	94
David,	95
Solomon,	95–100
Books of Chronicles,	100–104

(2) Poetical Books, ... 104–132

1. The Prophets.

Daniel,	105
Habbakuk,	105
Zephaniah,	105
Ezekiel,	105–107
Jeremiah,	107–112
Isaiah,	112–115
Micah,	115
Hosea,	115–121
Amos,	121–126
Joel,	126–127

ANALYTICAL INDEX.

PAGE

  2. Poems.
    Ecclesiastes, ... 127
    Solomon's Song, ... 127
    Proverbs, ... 128
    Psalms, ... 128–132
   Value of this Evidence, ... 132–134
 IV. *David to Moses*, ... 134–156
   1st Samuel, ... 134–141
   Judges, ... 141–142
   Joshua, ... 142–146
Observations on External Evidence, ... 146–151
Conclusion, ... 152–156

INTERNAL EVIDENCE.
 General Observations as to what would be the Character of the Books, supposing them to have been written at the Time claimed, 157–159
  I. Antiquity of Style, ... 159–176
  II. Contents and Structure. Removal of Unexpected Difficulties in the Laws, and Comparison of Numb. Lev. and Deut., ... 177–198
  III. Undesigned Coincidences, ... 198–208
  IV. Minuteness of Details, ... 208–215
  V. Chasms in the History, ... 216–217
  VI. References to Egyptian Customs, . . . 217–218
  VII. Adoption of Egyptian Words and Rites, 218–221
  VIII. No Evidences of Later Enactments, . . 221–223
  IX. Results, ... 223–225
  X. Conclusion.— Difficulties of Unbelief, . 226–230

www.ingramcontent.com/pod-product-compliance
Lightning Source LLC
Chambersburg PA
CBHW021939240426
43669CB00047B/550